Thomas Osborne Davis

**The Patriot Parliament of 1689**

With its statutes, votes, and proceedings

Thomas Osborne Davis

**The Patriot Parliament of 1689**
*With its statutes, votes, and proceedings*

ISBN/EAN: 9783337308094

Printed in Europe, USA, Canada, Australia, Japan

Cover: Foto ©Suzi / pixelio.de

More available books at **www.hansebooks.com**

THE
# PATRIOT PARLIAMENT
## OF 1689

*WITH ITS STATUTES VOTES AND PROCEEDINGS*

BY
THOMAS DAVIS

*EDITED WITH AN INTRODUCTION*
BY
THE HON. SIR CHARLES GAVAN DUFFY, K.C.M.G.

THIRD EDITION

London
T. FISHER UNWIN
PATERNOSTER SQUARE

| Dublin | New York |
|---|---|
| SEALY, BRYERS & WALKER | P. J. KENEDY |
| MIDDLE ABBEY STREET | BARCLAY STREET |

MDCCCXCIII

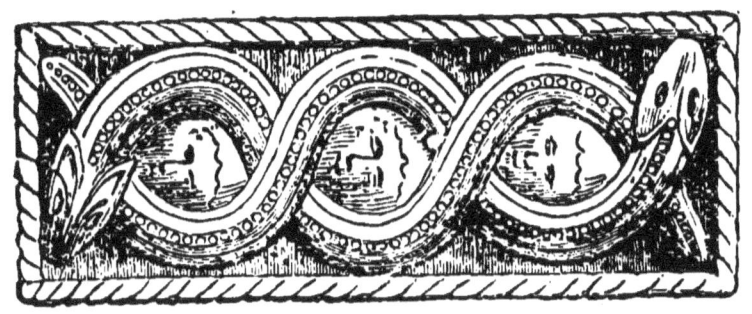

THE]
# EDITOR'S INTRODUCTION.

F this little book should fall into the hands of a reader to whom the name of the author, THOMAS DAVIS, is unfamiliar, he will certainly value the book more from knowing something of that remarkable man.

Davis was the youngest son of a family who were Protestants, and belonged to the party of Protestant ascendancy in Ireland,

and his father was an Englishman and an officer in the British army. But in early manhood he separated himself from these antecedents. The young man, during his college course, spent all his leisure not in indolence or enjoyment but in studying for himself the problems of Irish History; and when he came to understand them he was seized with the desire to make the truth known and recognised. On leaving college he became a barrister, but to serve his native country he relinquished his profession to work as a publicist in the National cause. He was one of the most upright and unselfish men whom it has been my good fortune to encounter in a long lifetime, and when he died in his thirty-first year, three years after this inquiry into James' Parliament was written, he left a name in Ireland which, among all the conflicting parties in that troubled country is a synonym of integrity and patriotism.

His judgment on one of the most debated of the Irish problems which he studied at college will be found in this volume. He has shown conclusively, I think, that the action of the "Popish Parliament of James II. in Ireland," so long and so shamefully misrepresented, was, to a notable degree, just, reasonable, and patriotic. He has further shown that the Irish Parliament was more moderate and honest, and essentially fairer, than the English Parliaments which preceded and followed it in order of time, or than the Protestant Parliament of Ireland which took its place after the Battle of the Boyne. I invite the reader to note that the identical offences charged on James's Catholic Parliament by partisan writers (and here disproved) were committed without shame or reserve by the Protestant Parliaments of the same era in both countries. That these two nations may understand each other and live at peace hereafter, nothing is more essential than that the wicked past should be understood and deplored.

Since Davis's death, Lord Macaulay has written a striking and persuasive, but essentially false account of James's transactions in Ireland. If that accomplished writer has treated no subject which he has not made luminous and attractive he has scarcely treated one in which a sober inquirer following in his track has not discovered that he habitually sacrificed truth to scenic effect, or in his history at any rate, to the predetermination to produce a national epic whose heroes were unchangeably in the right. There is an eminent living historian with a speciality for misrepresenting Irish affairs who has no more idea of fairness or reciprocity than a Mohawk; but many Irishmen prefer the naked enmity of Mr. Froude to the polished plausibility and disengenuous glosses of Lord Macaulay.

The transactions of the Irish Parliament

under the last of the Stuart kings will be imperfectly appreciated without some account of the previous relations of the princes of that ill-fated and ill-conducted house with the Irish people. James's brother, his father, and his grandfather had each helped to create a chaos which it was now the duty of a native parliament to reduce to order.

Let us begin with the achievements of his grandfather.

When the first Stuart king was called to the throne of England there was general rejoicing among the Catholics of Ireland. While he was still a pretender he had kept an agent in the camp of the Irish princes in arms against Elizabeth, he was son of Mary Queen of Scots regarded as a martyr for the Catholic Faith, and he was a prince of their own Milesian race. Now, it might be hoped, the country would have fair play, and, perhaps, a gleam of Court favour. But the English counsellors of James I.

knew that if he made concessions to Ireland he could scarce hold the English throne, and one of his earliest acts was a proclamation announcing that "liberty of conscience he could not grant." But though religious liberty must be refused, English law would be introduced to every part of the island, " the sword would be sheathed, and every man indiscriminately taken into the favour of the king's majestie."\* In that happy era the Irish were destined to learn how much more destructive an instrument than the sword that was sheathed is the inkhorn, when it is placed on the council-board to frame Acts of Parliament and Orders in Council. Though gallant adventurers could no longer, in the language of *Pacata Hibernia*, "have the killing of some Irish" as a morning's pastime, they might still, if they were skilful, enjoy much the same recreation, in the way of devising "beneficial measures" for the country.

\* Sir John Davies, Irish Attorney-General under James I.

In the transactions now to be briefly described, and which form the foundations of our modern history, English writers in general are agreed that the paramount nation exhibited singular wisdom and benevolence. Through constantly changing and troubled times they were always right; right when they did in Ireland the exact reverse of what they were accustomed to do at home; right, by a singular good fortune, when they set aside rules of morality and justice, which elsewhere are of permanent authority.

Lord Bacon, with whom ideas grew plentyfully, had a pregnant suggestion at the service of the king. He was of opinion that a great settlement of English husbandmen in Ireland able to guard as well as to till the land would help to secure the interest of the Crown. The only question was where to plant them. O'Neill and Tyrconnell had proved dangerous enemies to Elizabeth, and they possessed a fertile territory; but they had been ostentatiously received into favour at the close of the late reign, and some decent pretence for destroying them so soon was indispensable. It was found in a letter conveniently dropped in the precincts of Dublin Castle, disclosing a new conspiracy.

Of a conspiracy there was not then, and has not been since discovered, any evidence worth recording. The letter was probably forged according to the practice of the times; but where so noble a booty was to be distributed by the Crown, one can conceive how ill-timed and disloyal any doubt of their treason would have appeared at the Court of James, or of the Lord Deputy. They were proclaimed traitors, and fled to the Continent to solicit aid from the Catholic Powers. Without delay James and his counsellors set to work. The king applied to the City of London to take up the lands of the wild Irish. They were well watered, he assured them, plentifully supplied with fuel, with good store of all the necessaries for man's sustenance; and moreover, yielded timber, hides, tallow, canvas, and cordage for the purposes of commerce. The Companies of Skinners, Fishmongers, Haberdashers, Vintners and the like thereupon became Absentee Proprietors and have guzzled Irish rents in city feasts and holiday excursions to Ireland from that day to this. Six counties in Ulster were confiscated, and not merely the chiefs, but the entire population dispossessed. The fruitful plains of Armagh, the deep pastoral glens that lie between the sheltering hills of Donegal, the undulating meadow lands stretching by the noble lakes and rivers of Fermanagh, passed from the people which had possessed them since before the Redemption of mankind, to immigrants from England and Scotland.

It is not difficult to see in imagination the old race, broken by battle and suffering, and deprived, by a trick of state, of their hereditary chiefs, retiring slowly and with bitter hearts before the stranger. The alluvial lands were given to English courtiers whom the Scotch king found it necessary to placate, and to Scotch partisans whom he dared not reward in England. The peasants, driven out of the tribal lands to burrow in the hills or bogs, were not treated according to any law known among civilised men. Under Celtic tenure the treason of the chief, if he committed treason, affected them no more than the offences of a tenant for life affect a remainder man in our modern practice. Under the feudal system they were innocent feudatories who would pass with the forfeited land to the Crown, with all their personal rights undisturbed.

The method of settlement is stated with commendable simplicity by the latest historian, Mr. Froude. The "plantators" got all the land worth their having; what was not worth their having—the barren mountains and trackless morass, which after two centuries still in many cases yield no human food—were left to those who in the language of an Act of Parliament of the period were "natives of the realm of Irish blood, being descended from those who did inherit and possess the land." Lest the frugality of the Celts should enable them to peacefully regain some of their possessions, it was strictly conditioned that no plantator or servitor should alienate his portion, or any part thereof, "to the mere Irish." The confiscated territory amounted to two millions of acres. "Of these a million and a half," says Mr. Froude, "bog, forest and mountain were restored to the Irish. The half million acres of fertile land were settled with families of Scottish and English Protestants."

It was in this manner that the famous Plantation of Ulster was founded. The natives were discontented with these arrangements, and their perversity has been visited with passionate censure by indignant critics down to our own day. There is reason to believe, however, that if a settlement of Irish Catholics had been made in

England by Mary or James II., on whom the best lands of Norfolk and Suffolk, Essex and Sussex, Kent and Surrey, were bestowed, while the English were left only the forest, mountain, and morass, that just and temperate people would not have entirely approved of the transaction, and might even be tempted to call it in question when an opportunity offered.

The new colonists have been painted in unfavourable colours by critics not unfriendly to the plantation.* In many cases it is probable

---

* The picture drawn of their general character by Stewart, the son of one of the ministers who came over, is probably a little over-coloured, but there is no reason to doubt its substantial truth, and it does much to explain the ferocious character of the rebellion which followed. 'From Scotland came many, and from England not a few, yet all of them generally the scum of both nations, who from debt, or breaking or fleeing from justice, or seeking shelter, came hither, hoping to be without fear of man's justice, in a land where there was nothing, or but little as yet, of the fear of God. . . . On all hands Atheism increased, and disregard of God ; iniquity abounded, with contention, fighting, murder, adultery.'—Lecky's "History of England in the Eighteenth Century," vol. ii., p. 109.

they were stout soldiers or skilful husbandmen, who under more favourable conditions would have been an element of strength to the country. But the settlement had the fever of usurpation upon it. The rightful owners were forthcoming, and the planters held by no higher title than naked force; good as long as force was on their side, but not a moment longer. Fences were erected, fruit-trees planted, simple churches built, and after a time white-walled bawns rose in the midst of waving corn-fields and rosy orchards. It was a pleasant sight to see; but within a gunshot of the gay harvest and gardens, the remnant of the native race, to whom the land had descended since the Redemption, were pining in misery and bitter discontent. The barren hills or frozen bogs to which they were banished yielded little food except the milk of their kine. "The mountainy men," so the new settlers contemptuously named them, would have been more magnanimous than any race who have lived on this globe, if they acquiesced patiently in the transfer. They could not forget, any more than their kinsmen in the Scottish Highlands, that

> "The fertile plain, the softened vale,
> Were once the birthright of the Gael."*

If their efforts to "spoil the spoiler," and "from the robber rend his prey,"* do not thrill sympathetic boudoirs, and if the scenes of their exploits are not the annual haunt of sentimental tourists, it is not because the exploits were different from those so favoured, but because a Walter Scott has not yet arisen to interpret them to mankind.

To obtain the sanction of the Irish Parliament, composed of feudatories of the Crown, to the practice of transferring property from hereditary owners to foreign protégés of the reigning sovereign, would have been difficult under any

* Sir Walter Scott's "Lady of the Lake."

circumstances. But it was peculiarly difficult when the two races had just been declared equal in the eyes of the law, and some of the native chiefs sat with the old English and new English, and possessed an undoubted right to confirm or reject the royal scheme. But James was shown (by Bacon we may venture to surmise) a device for evading the difficulty, exactly suited to the temper of his mind, which he joyfully adopted. Forty boroughs were created in a single day, consisting for the most part of townships, where towns were projected but not built, or of groups of three or four houses inhabited by a dozen or so of new settlers, to whom in some cases a charter had not yet been issued. These boroughs were authorised to select two members each, and when the new Parliament met, two hundred thousand English and Anglo-Irish of the religion of the Court were found to have more representatives than the Irish nation, six times their number. The members for the new boroughs were not likely to be troublesome to the Crown; they were chosen from the Lord Deputy's servants, attorneys' clerks, bankrupts, outlaws, and other persons in a servile or dependent condition. The authentic representatives of the people sent agents to James to complain of this abuse of the royal prerogative by which they were swamped in their own Parliament by the intrusion of nearly eighty unauthorised persons. James returned an answer, which the reader may consider inadequate, but which would certainly have seemed sufficient to any Stuart that ever reigned in England. Too many members! "The more the merrier," quoth he, "the fewer the better cheer."

But Sir John Davies, Speaker of the new Parliament, was more politic than the king, and may indeed be regarded as the very high priest of plausibility in that day. He knew that the name and form of freedom had been granted to the nation, and clearly perceived that the form ought to be respected, though the substance might be skilfully filched away —a method of reforming Irish abuses which has never been permitted to fall into disuse. Under his direction the House of Commons confessed the wrong, but evaded the remedy. It was true that many members were "unduly elected," some (as the resolution recited) for "not being estated in their boroughs, some for being outlawed, excommunicated, and lastly, for being returned for places whose charters were not valid." It would greatly prejudice the public business, however, to create a delay just then; therefore the returns should not be questioned, but this resolution must, of course not be drawn into a precedent. The native members withdrew in a rage, and the representatives of the boroughs "whose charters were not valid," the bankrupt, outlawed, and excommunicated nominees of the Castle, declared the territory of O'Neill and O'Donnell forfeited to the Crown. Such a Parliament could scarcely be improved upon, and when leisure came the fraudulent boroughs were never called in question. They were not called in question, indeed, but carefully maintained by successive sovereigns and governments as a means of keeping Parliament in order, and the reader who is about to consider the Acts of James's Popish Parliament is invited to note these Acts of his grandfather's Protestant Parliament.

The next stroke of statesmanship which James adopted was worthy of its forerunners. When a Catholic proprietor died leaving children under age, the king like a true father of his people undertook the charge of the orphans. The powers and functions of the Court of Wards founded by Henry VIII. were enlarged, and as James could not get a wife out of Spain for his son, (on which condition, as we now all know, he was ready to "kiss the Pope's pantoufle,") he became an ardent Protestant, and it was ordered that the children should be strictly educated in the Reformed religion. If they were girls they were provided with Protestant husbands by James or Buckingham. This device proved a most successful stroke of State policy, and with the favours and blandishments of the Court judiciously distributed, did more than the laws of Henry and Elizabeth to win over the old families. Education is stronger than natural instincts or inherited opinions. The Janissaries were Christian orphans trained to be Mussulmen by the Sultan, and the most remorseless enemies of the Celt in the next generation were O'Briens and Butlers wards of the Crown strictly educated in the Reformed religion), who became more English than the English themselves.

In process of time the O'Brien became Earl of Thomond, the O'Healy, Earl of Donoghmore, the O'Quin, Earl of Dunraven, the O'Callaghan, Lord Lismore, the O'Neill, Lord O'Neill, and so forth; all partisans of the English interest, and the Established Church. The Anglo-Norman families went the same way; the Fitzgeralds, the Butlers, the De Courceys, the De Burgos, and the rest, made their submission to the State and the Church. From this time forth there were Irish courtiers in London. The chief, who lived among his people, and was a visible Providence, began to be replaced by an English cavalier who spent the revenue of the O'Brien's country, or the McWilliams's country, in playing hazard with Buckingham, or junketting with the accommodating ladies at Whitehall.

When Charles I. succeeded his father on the throne he was as eager to plant Irish lands with strangers as his predecessor. He was represented in Ireland by a trenchant Lord Deputy, remembered in that country as "Black Tom," and memorable in English history as Thomas Wentworth, Earl of Strafford. Wentworth resolved to make a settlement in Connaught to rival the settlement in Ulster. The first business was to clear out the owners in possession. The wildest inventions in "Candide," intended to illustrate human absurdity and wickedness, will not match the pretence on which the forfeiture of these estates was founded. In the previous reign when the king substituted "feudal tenure" for the Celtic system, the Connaught proprietors had duly submitted and paid him a heavy fine to have their new patents enrolled in Chancery. The officers of the Court, wilfully or ignorantly, omitted to make the proper entries in their books; and this misfeasance was declared by Court lawyers to have forfeited the lands of the province to the king. It is a maxim that no man can profit by his own fraud; but maxims are not made to bind sovereign princes. As the blessing of English law, however, had been extended to the whole nation, it was necessary that this opinion should be confirmed by the judgment of a Court and the verdict of a jury. If a dozen of his fellow-countrymen found a Connaught proprietor's title bad, calumny itself must be mute. Wentworth marched to the West at the head of formidable military force, as "good lookers-on," he said, and accompanied by the necessary retinue of judges and lawyers to perform the judicial ceremony. Some of the juries were frightened into verdicts; some were wheedled into them, for to sharpen the persuasive power of the judges Wentworth secretly gave these learned personages a percentage on the forfeitures. But in Galway the juries were of opinion that, notwithstanding the misconduct of the officers of Chancery, the land did not belong to the king, but to the owners, and they found accordingly. Wentworth's method of encountering this difficulty may help to mitigate our surprise that the Irish people did not cordially love a system of jurisprudence which has undeniably secured equal justice to many generations of Englishmen. The jurors who found a verdict according to their conscience, and not according to the wishes of the Lord Deputy, were immediately brought before the Castle Chamber in Dublin, and fined £4,000 each and their estates seized till the fine was paid; a penalty the equivalent of which would impoverish many a noble of the present day. They were further required to acknowledge their offence in public court on bended knees. The lawyers who had the wickedness to plead for the native proprietors were tendered the Oath of Supremacy, which as Catholics they could not take; and declining to take it were excluded from future practice. The sheriff who summoned the jurors was dealt with in a more decisive fashion; he was first fined and then flung into prison, where he was kept till he died of the process; an example to future officials to array their panels more discreetly.

If these excesses seem impossible it may be noted that the London Parliament on the occasion of Strafford's impeachment, cited among the catalogue of his achievements in Ireland—" that jurors who gave their verdict according to their consciences, were censured in the Castle Chamber in great fines; sometimes pilloried, with loss of ears, and bored through the tongue, and sometimes marked in the forehead, with other infamous punishments."

Though the character of Charles I. as a compound of egotism and faithlessness is one of the most familiar studies in English history, it may borrow a characteristic touch from Irish records. Before these transactions he appealed in sore stress to his Irish subjects for a grant of money; the Catholics took his wants into consideration and offered a subsidy of £120,000—an enormous sum in that day—provided that no proprietor sixty years in undisturbed possession should be troubled respecting his title; and that

Catholics should be allowed to practice as barristers without taking the oath of supremacy. Charles took the money, and promised the "Graces" (so they were named) which the Catholics desired. The Puritans, however, grew daily stronger, and to keep the promise of tolerating Papists, even in so small a matter as not cheating them out of their estates, soon became inconvenient. Some of the bishops of the Irish Establishment transmitted a fierce remonstrance to England against any concession to Catholics, and as Charles was a good Churchman and loved his bishops, he was sorely perplexed; but above all there was the glory and profit of making a plantation in Connaught no longer possible if he kept his word.* Wentworth saw an easy way out of

* The protest of the bishops drawn up by Archbishop Ussher, one of the ablest men the Irish Establishment has produced, is commended to the attention of persons who are accustomed to clamour about the bigotry of Rome. "The Religion of the Papists is Superstitious and Idola-

the difficulty; let him not keep his promise; and he, for his part, was willing to assist so worthy a purpose by bearing all the blame. Charles's whole character is painted in the two trous, their Faith and Doctrines erroneous and heretical, their Church, in respect of both, Apostatical: to give them, therefore, a *Toleration*, or to consent that they may, freely, exercise their Religion, and profess their Faith and Doctrine, is a grievous sin."

The principle which lay at the root of this persecuting spirit is curious. The Puritans insisted upon the right of private judgment. They were fighting for religious freedom against a persecuting king. Independents, Anabaptists, and Brownists were not to be disturbed in their liberty of conscience. To set up a new creed in a new conventicle was lawful. But if a man's private judgment led him to prefer the faith that prevailed throughout the bulk of Christendom, then the rule did not apply.

Lord Macaulay, who seems always to have proceeded upon the assumption that justice is a luxury, like Bass's beer and Holloway's ointment, intended specially for British enjoyment, says of this era: "One part of the empire was so unhappily circumstanced that, at that time, its misery was necessary to our happiness, and its slavery to our freedom."* This maxim describes the policy to which Lord Macaulay himself was a party in the reign of Queen Victoria as accurately as Cromwell's in the Commonwealth; and to my thinking, is as base a rule of conduct as any that can be picked out of Macchiavelli.

* In the *Edinburgh Review* article "Milton."

facts, that he broke his promise without scruple, after he had spent the subsidy, and thankfully accepted Strafford's offer to stand between him and the infamy he had incurred. He even improved in time on the teaching of his minister. Later, when the Puritans determined to destroy Strafford himself, the king passionately assured him that not a hair of his head would he suffer to be touched; but when he discovered that it would be dangerous to keep his word, he graciously pronounced the ceremonial "Le roi le veut" over the Act of Parliament which sent Strafford to the block; a transaction in which the student will probably recognise what is called poetic justice.

Nearly a generation had elapsed since the Plantation of Ulster, when the troubles between Charles and his Parliament began. The middle classes and many of the gentry distrusted his policy in Church and State, and feared his leanings towards Rome. They had some ground for their fears. His wife was a devout Catholic; his chief adviser in spiritual affairs, Archbishop Laud, was a High Churchman, to whom a Catholic was more acceptable than a Sectary; and to Charles himself, Rome was not so odious as Geneva. By this time a great change had come over the English people. They had grown graver and more thoughtful than at the era of the Reformation. As soon as the stern authority of Henry was removed, a sect sprang up which aimed to model the new Church on the doctrine and system of Calvin. From the strictness of their tenets, and the severity of their practices, they were named, partly in ridicule, the Puritans. These men were more in earnest than the courtly ecclesiastics, and more intelligible to the people, and their opinions spread rapidly, chiefly among the industrious class, as Wesleyan Methodism spread in a later age, for the same reason. They had embarrassed James by questions of prerogative, and they set up a fierce parliamentary opposition as often as want of money compelled Charles to summon a parliament. John Pym, John Hampden, and other men of remarkable ability, led this party, and it soon became plain that the issue would be civil war. The Puritans were undoubtedly contending for liberty, but it was liberty in which Prelatists and Papists should have no share. Their success has been a blessing to mankind; but it is a blessing because mankind have peremptorily rejected many of the perverted opinions which distinguished the Puritans from the rest of the nation.

Secretly instigated by the Parliamentary leaders, the Scots rose against the king and invaded England in considerable force, and Charles summoned to his aid the army which Wentworth maintained in Ireland; an army recruited in part from Irish Catholics. In the House of Commons this project evoked a storm of resistance. It was permissible to call a Scottish army into England, and it was a natural right, which no one would be mad enough to dispute, to send an English army into Ireland, but if an Irish army were brought into England, on any pretence whatever, that was an outrage sufficient to release subjects from their allegiance. The Irish, who did not quite see the force of this distinction, began to bestir themselves. They heard of threats in London that Popery must be extirpated; Pym, in the House of Commons, boasted, it was said, that Parliament would not leave a Papist in Ireland; they noted the successful rebellion of the Scots, they saw their old enemies in conflict, and the time seemed propitious to regain their ancient lands, and to save such as remained from bribed judges and panic-stricken juries. Roger O'Moore, a man greatly gifted both to project and to persuade, and whom contemporaries of all parties pronounce of unblemished honour, brought leading men together, kindled them with his own convictions, and in a short time there was a genuine conspiracy on foot to seize the seat of government, and summon the Irish race to arms. For now again there had risen among the Irish race a Statesman; one who not only recognised injustice and pitied it, of which sort there was never any scarcity, but one who saw how to amend or end it.

Owen Connolly, servant of one of the conspirators, betrayed his master, several of the leaders were seized, and the Government in Dublin put effectually on their guard. But the North was beyond their control. There the clans who had been pillaged by James, or their immediate descendants, rose on an autumn night forty thousand strong, led by Sir Phelim (still remembered by Ulster peasants as Phelemy) O'Neill and other chiefs of their own blood, drove out the English and Scotch settlers, and repossessed themselves of their ancient tribal lands. This is the transaction known to English writers as the "Great Popish Rebellion," and the "Popish Massacre;" the leader of the rising being a man educated by the Court of Wards as a Protestant. By whatever contumelious nickname it may be branded, what happened in Ireland is what would happen under similar conditions in any branch of the human family. When a favourable opportunity offered they " spoiled the spoiler." So the Saxons dealt with their Norman conquerors, as far as their power and opportunity permitted, and the Dutch with their Spanish conquerors, and the Sicilians with their French conquerors. Though there were dreadful excesses committed by both parties in the end, it is certain beyond all controversy, that the first aim of the Irish was to regain their own without any sacrifice of life. On the night of the rising, and during the six days that followed, only one man was killed; a fact which stamps with complete certainty their original purpose. When blood is shed it is like kindling the prairie; no one can any longer pretend to limit the devastation. But there were some signal instances of moderation; certain priests it is recorded concealed fugitives under their altars; and Dr. Bedell, a bishop of the Protestant Establishment, who had distinguished himself by humane conduct in his day of power, was permitted in the very focus of the insurrection, to fill his house with English settlers, and shelter them from all molestation.

The contemporary accounts of the transaction are quite as untrustworthy as the narratives of Titus Oates and his confederates. The settlers depended absolutely on the support of England for maintaining their position. Many of them had suffered grievously, and the remainder were in danger of losing the fruit of all their toil and enterprise. What sort of stories they sent to Westminster under such circumstances, to inflame the zeal of their partizans, may be conceived. All Puritan England was ready to believe, and eager to hear, new marvels of Irish iniquity. Pious tears and rage were excited by a description of the ghosts of murdered Protestants appearing in broad daylight, day after day, on the bridge of Portadown, (where unhappily a settlement was cruelly destroyed,) wringing their hands and uttering piercing shrieks for an avenger. One peculiarly stubborn ghost held his ground for more than a month. A bishop was among the witnesses of these impressive facts; which exhibited, as one can conceive heaven itself among the allies of the plantators.*

The broad sheets published in London from day to day, by the Parliament and its partisans, were as shameless as the inventions of a Hindoo

* There is in Trinity College, Dublin, a mass of depositions intended to establish these astonishing phenomena, and others nearly as marvellous. Edmund Burke, who personally examined the documents, speaks of the "rascally collection" in the College, relative to the pretended massacre of 1641. Mr. Froude (among many smaller Froudes) of course accepts this "rascally collection" as if they were so many proofs of Holy Writ.

against a fallen enemy. But they did their work. They fed the prejudice of the English people against the "Queen's Party," and to this hour they are the familiar materials of English History. The best of them is abundantly leavened with falsehood, but some of them must have been invented in London, for no plantator would have ventured on fabrications so glaring and palpable. Among prominent leaders of the rebels, for example, we find the illustrious potentates Lords Matquers, Dulon, Don Lace Cargena, Limbrey, and Lewricole. These great unknown or their followers, committed excesses in districts of commensurate obscurity. They burned Lognall, and Toyhull ; seized upon fifteen towns in the great county of Monno (by some read Conno), laid siege to Anney, and committed unheard of cruelties in the populous and Protestant county of Warthedeflowr. In some of them Dublin is seized by the natives, in others O'Neill is a prisoner in the hands of the Irish Government. One Tract contains a a circumstantial account by " One of God's ministers" of a new gunpowder plot, to blow up the flourishing town of Rockoll, six miles from Dublin, while the king's army were in the act of passing through it; but fortunately this atrocity was prevented by the gallant conduct of a gentleman of whom posterity has been singularly unmindful, Mr. Carot Topey.*

The theory finally adopted by English and Anglo-Irish writers generally, with respect to this transaction, when the clouds of prejudice and misrepresentation had blown away, is perplexing to human reason. To seize the hereditary lands of the Irish race, and drive out the inhabitants from the pastoral valleys and alluvial plains which they and theirs had enjoyed since the dawn of history, was a wise stroke of states-

* See Thorpe's Tracts, a collection of contemporary brochures, in the Royal Irish Academy, Dublin, collected and presented by Mr. Thorpe.

manship it seems ; but to seize the same lands occupied for a single generation by English settlers, and drive out the inhabitants, in order to place the original population in their own possessions, was a crime of incredible greed and cruelty. A title founded on the naked ground of conquest is necessarily liable to the right of resumption or reconquest, which establishes a similar title in some other persons. Six years earlier the Scotch had risen in defence of their religion, and for the redress of civil grievances. And they succeeded. No person has yet suggested an intelligible reason why the Irish also should *not* defend their religion, and procure the redress of grievances. In modern times, when the original history of the massacre is well understood to have been partly a scare, partly a lie, the chief complaint against the Irish is that they laid waste a flourishing settlement where goodly men were enjoying the fruits of their industry in holy peace. But the contemporary evidence is of a different character. The last glimpse we catch of the Scotch plantators exhibits them enduring, from English bishops and nobles, the same stripes which Dundee and Dalzell inflicted on Cameronians and Covenanters a generation later—reduced to such a plight indeed that there would seem but little left for the Irish enemy to do. In a petition to the English Commons in 1640, the Presbyterians of Antrim, Down, and Tyrone, declare that by "the cruelties, severities and arbitrarie proceedings of civil magistrates, but principally through the sway of the prelacy with their faction, our souls are starved, our estates undone, our families empoverished, and many lives among us cut off and destroyed." They summed up the result. "Our cruel taskmasters have made us, who were once a people, to become, as it were, no people, an astonishment to ourselves, the object of pittie and amazement to others."*

* Humble Petition of the Protestants, etc. Thorpe's "Tracts"

The array of authorities for the common English view of the rising is very imposing, having the august name of John Milton at its head. But it is not more certain that Titus Oates' story of the Popish Plot was a fabrication, than that John Milton's specific statements about the Irish rebellion were unfounded and impossible. He placed the number of the massacred at 616,000, the Protestant population of the island, including soldiers in garrison and officials in Dublin, and the great towns, amounting at that time to little over 200,000. Temple, who is the unrelenting enemy of the Irish, estimates the slain in his history of the transaction, at 150,000; and Clarendon, the royalist historian, reduces it to 50,000. These were guesses more or less wild. Cromwell issued a commission to investigate the wrongs endured by the British in Ireland, and Cromwell's commission, before which the maddest evidence was produced, and where the same incident is reported by various witnesses, and counted over and over, fixes the number of murders at 2,109, to which 1,900 cases, supposed to have occurred during the Confederate war, are added. If we accept as authentic the report of a fanatical commission, before whom no evidence on the part of the Irish was heard, and who believed in ghosts shrieking in the broad day for a Protestant avenger, Milton multiplied every murder by more than 100. Fairly judged at this day it must be admitted that the transfer of the land back to its original owners was made with as little premeditated violence as in any agrarian revolution with which it can be fairly brought into comparison. Bloody reprisals were the custom of the age; in the Netherlands, in Italy, and in France, the faction of the Catholics and the faction of the Reformers killed and ravaged. without remorse. That a race whose chiefs had been trapped like wild beasts, or assassinated in the very offices of hospitality, among whom the tragedy of the *Pacata Hibernia*, and the kindred tragedy of the Plantation of Ulster, were performed, should have been stung into no deadlier a humour will be for ever a marvel to men who have studied human history and human nature. The outrages shamefully exaggerated were no part of the original design. The rising, when it fell under the guidance of Roger O'Moore, finally swelled into a revolution, had its parliament at Kilkenny, to which Charles sent ambassadors, and its armies in the field, to which in the end he would gladly have committed his cause, and conducted its measures with notable clemency and moderation.*

* Unless on the hypothesis that there is a separate scheme of divine and human justice, and a separate law of nature, applicable to Ireland, it is difficult to account for the contradictory judgment which a man ordinarily so wise and just as Mr. Carlyle, applies to nearly identical circumstances in Ireland and France. In Ireland the agricultural population driven wild by pillage and oppression, rose and repossessed themselves of lands

At the period of the Rising, the Lords Justices were Sir John Parsons and Sir John Borlase. Parsons, who was one of the greediest and most unscrupulous adventurers of whom history has left a record, was the leading spirit. He pursued with brutal frankness the policy which had secretly influenced the statesmen of the Pale at every critical era since the Invasion; he aimed to make peace impossible that forfeited estates might be plentiful. The Catholic peers and gentlemen of English descent had little national

recently taken from them, and in the process committed and endured cruel excesses: in France the agricultural population, also long oppressed and pillaged, rose and burned the chateaux of the noblesse, who had possessed them for centuries, killed the owners whenever they could find them, and when their partisans were in prison rose in conjunction with a city mob and murdered them in cold blood. Of the Irish transaction Mr. Carlyle has written a vehement and unmeasured condemnation. Of the French massacre he says: " Horrible in lands that had known equal justice. Not so unnatural in lands that had never known it. *Le sang qui coule est il donc si pur?* asks Barnave, intimating that the gallows, though by irregular methods, had its own."—Carlyle's "French Revolution."

spirit, and some of them were ready to prove their loyalty by taking up arms against the Northern Irish. But Parsons and his associates at the Privy Council determined to treat all Papists on the same footing. They were disarmed indiscriminately. A few wished to retire to England, but permission was refused. They were ordered to reside on their estates, and not to return to Dublin on pain of death. That living at home might not be unduly agreeable, they were forbidden to retain the arms necessary for the defence of their houses against marauders. Some whom he choose to suspect were put to the torture to extract a confession of their complicity with O'Neill. In short he left them no choice but to fight in self-defence, and at length they took up arms. Certain priests had distinguished themselves, as we have seen, in protecting the English fugitives in the North, and the Council checked this dangerous practice by ordering that all priests who fell into the hands of the army should be forthwith put to death. The English Parliament highly approved of these measures, and solemnly resolved that no toleration should thenceforth be given to Popery in Ireland. To give full effect to their determination a loan was raised upon two millions and a half of "profitable lands," which it was agreed to take from the owners and sell to English adventurers.

In the Irish Parliament, known as the Confederation of Kilkenny, the Catholics of both races were fully represented. Don Eugenio O'Neill, known in Irish annals as Owen Roe,* a soldier who had acquired skill and experience in the armies of Spain, came to the aid of his countrymen. The Confederation established a regular government under the title of the Supreme Council, got an army into the field in each of the four provinces, coined money, sent agents to Rome and to the great Catholic powers, issued

* Red Owen, so called from the colour of his hair.

letters of marque to privateers, and established free trade with the Continent, from which arms and ammunition were obtained plentifully. It was not the least of its achievements that it set up a printing press, a machine so rare, and so restricted by law, that there was but one in Ireland, that one in use at the seat of English government in Dublin.

The war which the Confederation maintained was distinguished by clemency and good faith. They were apparently determined that the national cause, represented by the leading men of the nation, should be clearly distinguishable from the rising of plundered peasants in the North; and it will be so distinguished by fair critics for ever. When strong places fell into their hands they murdered no garrisons, sacked no cities, burned no churches, put no peaceful inhabitants to the sword, though these crimes were being committed against them at the moment. The English Parliament directed that all Irish Papists fighting for the king in Scotland (where the Catholics had sent Charles some aid), or at sea, should be denied quarter, and Irish soldiers were strung up in batches, and their wives and children flung into the sea in pursuance of this order. If the Catholics had retaliated who could be surprised; but the Supreme Council forbade retaliation. In the first year of the war the garrison of Drogheda received the submission of 1,200 Protestants, who were admitted to terms and treated with humanity. And this was their common custom. They practised forbearance to lengths, which, in face of the provocation they endured, was amazing and admirable. For the soldiers of the Parliament fought under the inspiration of men who declared that one Papist must not be left in Ireland. The most ferocious of these soldiers was Sir Charles Coote. His career is an unbroken record of murder and plunder. We read of garrisons put to the sword after they had laid down their arms, of towns, villages, and manor houses wantonly burned, of growing crops laid waste, of priests and friars knocked on the head whenever they were encountered all told as coolly as a modern reporter describes a battue; till at length a musket ball brought his achievements to a sudden end. Monroe, a Scotch soldier, rivalled Coote in barbarity; he is described as roasting fugitives—many hundred it is alleged—in a wood, which he fired to destroy them—laying waste the harvest and renewing the other horrors of the *Pacata Hibernia*, till happily he encountered Owen Roe, as we shall see. Lord Inchiquin, the head of a family which inherited the blood of Brian Borhoime, has left a blacker memory than Coote or Monroe. He is still execrated in Munster as Murrogh of the Burnings. The achievement by which he is best remembered is the sacking of the ancient church on the

Rock of Cashel. He offered terms, it is said, to the garrison empowering them to depart with all the honours of war, but they refused to leave the priests and citizens at his mercy. A prodigious slaughter ensued; when the struggle was over nearly a thousand dead bodies of the besieged and besiegers (for the garrison fought gallantly) strewed the church and its approaches. Twenty priests were massacred, and one of their confreres has left this vivid picture of the scenes which ensued: "The altars were overturned; the images that were painted on wood were consigned to the flames; those on canvas were used as bedding for the horses, or were cut into sacks for burdens. The great crucifix which stood at the entrance of the choir, as if it had been guilty of treason, was beheaded, and soon after its hands and feet were amputated. With a like fury did they rage against all the other chapels of the city; gathering together the sacred vases and all the most precious vestments, they formed a procession in ridicule of our ceremonies. They marched through the public squares, wearing the sacred vestments, having the priests' caps on their heads, and inviting to Mass those whom they met on the way. A beautiful statue of the Immaculate Virgin taken from our church was borne along (the head being broken off) in mock state, with laughter and ridicule. The leader of the Puritan army had the temerity to assume the archiespicopal mitre, and boast that he was now not only governor and lieutenant of Munster, but also Archbishop of Cashel."*

The Confederate Council ordered that "accurate accounts" of these outrages should be collected. Strict accuracy was scarcely to be expected under the circumstances; the accounts were afterwards published, and it may well be that they were exaggerated by

* Narrative of the Irish Superior of the Jesuits, cited in Cardinal Moran's Persecution of the Irish Catholics.

rage and horror; but they rested, I do not doubt, on a substantial basis of truth. They can scarcely be matched, in human annals, for cold blooded and wanton cruelty. They record the burning of aged men and women, the murder of the blind and disabled, of women who bore other lives, and the drowning of batches of unarmed peasants with their wives and little ones. Two hundred women and children, they alleged, were smothered in a cave in Donegal; three hundred men, women and children who sought shelter in Derry were butchered by the garrison; five hundred persons were arrested by soldiers at Newry and flung in successive batches into the river; Irish soldiers who yielded on terms at Clongowswood, were hung as soon as they had submitted; and a hundred and fifty women and children (camp followers it may be presumed), slaughtered; three hundred peaceful farmers and farm labourers with their families were murdered by the Parliamentarians quartered in Drogheda; eighty-eight inhabitants of Bandon were tied back to back and flung into the river by the garrison (the same garrison are described in another of their slaughter houses as seizing young children by the legs and knocking their brains out against the wall), a hundred and fifty persons of both sexes at Termonfechan were roasted to death by setting fire to a furze-cover in which they had taken shelter. And so forth through a long catalogue of cruelty and perfidy; but the task of recalling these bitter memories is odious, and I stop midway. They might, perhaps, be forgotten,—they might, at least, have vanished from the popular memory, had they had no successors. But what Irish boy has not conversed with men who saw crimes as shameful and inhuman committed in Wexford and Carlow at the end of the last century? Crimes for ever renewed cannot be forgotten; they are indispensable materials of history, for they have largely contributed to form the Irish character as it exists at this day.*

The Pope sent a nuncio to aid the Irish with his advice, and with some help in money and arms. Irish officers returned in considerable numbers from France, Italy, and Spain, and

---

* The Rev. Dr. Leland, a Professor in Trinity College, Dublin, and a Chaplain to the Lord Lieutenant, describes an incident of another character in the war worthy to live as long as the story of Regulus:

"The Romish Bishop of Ross, who had been particularly active in raising and animating these unfortunate troops, was taken prisoner in the engagement. A man so distinguished in his opposition to the parliamentarians could expect no mercy; Broghill, however, promised to spare his life, on condition that he should use his spiritual authority with the garrison of a fort adjacent to the field of battle, and prevail them to surrender. For this purpose he was conducted to the fort; but the gallant captive, unshaken by the fear of death, exhorted the garrison to maintain their post resolutely against the enemies of their religion and their country, and instantly resigned himself to execution. His enemies could discover nothing in this conduct but insolence and obstinacy, for he was a Papist and a Prelate."

INTRODUCTION. lvii

brought, we may assume, a deposit of arms which, according to an English spy, these gallant exiles had long before " bought out of the deduction of their pay," in hopes of some such opportunity. Richelieu meditated sending officers and money, perhaps a French expedition to Ireland, when death cut short his memorable career. The war continued for seven years ; and in the end the success of the Confederates, and his own repeated defeats in England, induced Charles to open negotiations with the Catholics and propose terms securing them religious liberty, and .a fair share of political power in their own country. The faithlessness which marked his entire history, however, lost him his last friends. He was impatient for Irish help to regain his position, but he meant to buy it a bargain. " I do, therefore, command you," he wrote to the Lord Lieutenant, " to conclude a peace with the Irish, whate're it cost, so that my Protestant subjects there may be secured, and my regal authority preserved. But for all this, you are to make the best bargain you can, and not to discover your enlargement of power till you needs must; and though I leave the managing of this great and necessary work entirely to you, yet I cannot but tell you, that if the suspension of Poining's Act for such bills as shall be agreed upon between you there, and the present taking away of the Penal laws against Papists by a law will do it, I shall not think it a bad bargain, so that freely and vigorously they engage themselves in my assistance against my rebels of England and Scotland, for which no conditions can be too hard, not being against conscience and honour."

The Catholics who remembered Charles's double dealing about the "Graces" were not prepared to pay him in advance a second time. If they set him up again in England, he must set them up in religious and political equality in their own country. It was a fair proposal;

but so little was Charles's agent, the Duke of Ormond, disposed to second it that he gave up Dublin to the Parliament (on excellent terms for himself personally), and left the country rather than assent. The king, pressed by his increasing danger in England, despatched a Catholic nobleman to the Confederation bearing an affectionate private letter from Charles to the nuncio, and a public despatch conceding all that was asked. But the unhappy faithless prince at the same time privately wrote to Ormond, " Be not startled at my great concessions to Ireland, for *they will come to nothing.*"

Among the Catholic leaders of that era the name of Owen Roe is the one name that still lives in popular love and traditiona reverence. Owen's most memorable achievement was a great victory over a parliamentary army at Benburb. The loss of the Puritans, mostly Scots, with Ulster planters for auxiliaries and led by the ferocious Monroe, was prodigious.

More than twenty officers were killed, and as many as 3,200 of the rank and file; over thirty standards, and the great guns, ammunition, and equipment of a camp, fell into the hands of O'Neill, whose loss in killed and wounded did not amount to quite 200 men. But in a subsequent campaign a fatal calamity fell on the Irish cause in the sudden death of Owen.* After that event the war, which had been maintained through seven stormy years with varying fortune prospered no more. The Catholics, though they still held the chief towns in Munster and Connaught, attained none of the objects for which they were in arms. But let us remember that though unsuccessful they were fighting for freedom of conscience, as the Scots at the same time were fighting for it; as the Dutch, some-

* It was widely believed that Owen was poisoned by a treacherous gift from a Puritan lady (after the practice of the previous century, when it is admitted that Elizabeth countenanced the poisoning of Irish leaders), but no evidence to justify this suspicion has ever been exhibited.

what earlier, had fought for it. They did not succeed in escaping from bondage, but the wrath of their keepers at the attempt deserves the sympathy of mankind in the same measure as the rage of a slave-driver whose tranquillity has been disturbed by unexpected resistance to the lash.

When Charles was deposed and executed Cromwell carried his victorious army across the Channel to conquer Ireland for the Commonwealth. His campaign was as coldly merciless as was Alva's in the Netherlands, or Carew's in Desmond. We are assured on high authority that he was in truth a humane and beneficent ruler, who only struck hard because it was necessary to execute Divine justice on the authors of the Ulster Rising. In pursuance of this meritorious policy he besieged Drogheda, which was held for the king, and put to the sword the entire garrison, and the population of all ages and both sexes; nobody being spared.

The massacre continued for several days; it is admitted that between three and four thousand persons were butchered in cold blood; and a score or two of the inhabitants, who alone escaped, were sold as slaves to the tobacco plantations. Among the garrison was an English regiment, commanded by an English Cavalier, and as Drogheda always lay within the English Pale, where the native Irish were long forbidden to inhabit a walled town, the traders and citizens were almost without exception Catholics of English blood. What Cromwell actually did was to kill certain Englishmen and Anglo-Irishmen in order to punish the imputed offences of O'Neills and O'Reillys, Maguires and MacMahons. The account of the transaction which he sent to England was that it was a righteous judgment executed "on the barbarous wretches who had imbued their hands in so much innocent blood." He repeated the lesson of Divine justice at

# INTRODUCTION. lxiii

Wexford. There the garrison and population were Irish, but Irish of the South; there is no reason to believe that it contained one soldier or citizen who had ever crossed the Boyne, or been any more associated with Sir Phelim O'Neill than with Praise God Barebones. The English Parliament ordered a general public thanksgiving throughout the whole nation for the happy event at Drogheda.

Charles II. was invited to take personal command of the native army in Ireland. He sent them assurances of sympathy, and confirmed the concessions to Catholics made by his father. But he preferred relying on his countrymen the Scots, who accepted him as their king, on conditions which made him infamous, and destroyed his last chance in Ireland. He had to subscribe the Covenant against Papists and Prelatists and to publish a declaration acknowledging his father's sin in having married his mother—"an idolatrous woman"—and in having made peace with the Irish Papists ; which peace since his father's death, he had himself acknowledged and confirmed. When these proceedings became known there was an end to the royal cause in Ireland. Charles took the earliest opportunity to send private assurances to the Catholics that he only made these professions for convenience, and under duresse ; but his father had exhausted this device, and garrison after garrison submitted to the Commonwealth.

It must never be forgotten that the troops of the Confederation, during the entire war, did not put one man to death in cold blood. The troops of the Parliament, when the contest was practically at an end, shot general officers as if they were banditti—among others the son of Owen Roe, and Heber MacMahon, Bishop of Clogher, who succeeded Owen as commander-in-chief. Of rank and file they slaughtered, during the war, ten times the number who had fallen in the Rising. And there are incidents in that remorseless campaign which might move the pity of Marat or St. Just.

Cromwell was now undisputed master, and a period followed which we are exhorted to recognise as the sole era when an authentic God-given ruler made Divine justice prevail in the land. Of his Divine government of Ireland the naked facts are these: Two years after the war was at an end, and when the fighting men of Ireland to the number of 40,000 had been encouraged to take service with Spain, he drove out by beat of drum the entire Catholic population of three provinces, excepting only hinds useful to hold the plough or herd the flocks of the conqueror. Aged men and women, feeble and sickly persons, many who were protected by general treaties, others who were protected by special terms of submission, some who had received personal guarantees for personal services, were driven across the Shannon, to find a shelter if they could in the bogs of Connaught, and their lands

E

divided among his soldiery. Peers and knights who had fought for the king, to whom they had sworn allegiance, were held by the representative of Divine justice to have incurred this penalty. If they returned they became liable to be hanged without trial. Of the labouring classes all who were considered dangerous, were treated with a barbarity beside which Louis Napoleon's deportation of his political enemies to Cayenne, in our own day, was mild. They were seized upon, and sold into perpetual slavery in the West Indies, at so much a head; five and twenty pounds being the average price which the Commonwealth obtained for an Irish slave. Twenty thousand men, and a large number of women (said to be chiefly the wives of soldiers who had been induced to enlist in foreign service), were so transported and sold. Youngsters, who cannot be considered guilty of any offence, shared the same fate. By the direct agency of Cromwell's son a rape, like Herod's, was committed on the children of the poorer classes, of whom he caused 1,000 boys to be sold as slaves, and 1,000 innocent Irish girls to be sent to Jamaica, to a fate which would scarcely be adequately avenged if the authentic ruler spent an eternity in the region to which Cavalier toasts consigned him. The admitted aim of the Lord Protector was to extirpate the Irish race, and his policy is still known among them as the "Curse of Cromwell." If this be indeed the art of Divine government, it was afterwards practised more successfully in the *fusillades* and *noyades* of the French Jacobins, and in the Bulgarian atrocities painted by a modern statesman ; and it reaches its perfection in the management of a prize by pirates, when the crew are made to walk the plank, and the booty distributed among the victors. Cromwell's conduct is still defended on the same fanatical pretences employed to justify the expulsion of the Huguenots from France, the Moors from Spain, the Jews from Russia, and the Christians from Japan, and the justification is good for all these transactions, or for none of them.

There was probably not one member of James's Irish Parliament to whom these events were not as well known as the names of his own children; and in judging the character of that assembly this fact ought never to be left out of account.

Before Cromwell's policy was carried to complete success the Restoration brought back the Stuarts. Charles II. having compensated or reinstated a host of royalists ejected from their estates in England, turned his attention to Ireland. The enemies of his house were in possession of the lands confiscated under Cromwell, and the friends of his house, the original proprietors, who were the last to lay down arms for his father, some of whom had shared his own exile, were in penury and destitution. The king who never said a foolish thing, and never did a wise (or honest) one, was ready enough to acknowledge the service of the Irish, if that would suffice. " In the last place we did and must always remember, the great affection a considerable part of that nation expressed to us, during the time of our being beyond the seas when with all ˙cheerfulness and obedience, they received and submitted to our orders, and betook themselves to that service which we directed as most convenient and behoofeful, at the time to us, though attended with inconvenience enough to themselves, which demeanour of theirs cannot but be thought very worthy of our protection, justice and favour." But compliments would *not* suffice. It was a case needing prompt handling, and Charles handled it with unusual promptitude. To pacify the Irish Puritans he confirmed the settlement of property under the Commonwealth. That is to say, Cromwell had given to his soldiers the estates of the Catholic gentlemen who had fought for the house of Stuart, and the restored house of Stuart graciously confirmed the arrangement. Charles would certainly have preferred doing justice, if justice could be done without too much personal inconvenience. But he loved his harlots and jesters too well to run risks; and to do justice in this matter was made difficult by a sentiment always powerful in England; a sentiment which has created a perpetual barrier between the two nations, and which while it exists will never suffer them to unite. His English Parliament, crowded with Cavaliers and returned exiles, would not have helped him to displace Englishmen, though they were Cromwellians, to make place for Irishmen, though they were Royalists. His impulse to do justice, indeed, was at best not very strong; a slice of confiscated land remained at the disposal of the Crown, with which he might have made a provision for a few more of the worst cases of injustice; but his heart was touched with fraternal affection, and he gave the bulk of it—a hundred and seventy thousand acres and upwards—not to Irish sufferers, but to his brother James—the same James whose Irish legislation is under inquiry in the following paper:

Charles' confirmation of the Cromwellian grants was known as the Act of Settlement, and the crime of James's Irish Parliament most clamorously denounced by English historians was their repeal of that shameful Act.

Although the Cavalier Parliament did not give back their estates to its Irish allies, it is needless to say that it did not quite overlook them. It compelled the king to withdraw a rash indulgence by which they were permitted to practise their religion. It passed a Test Act, by which no person could hold any office, civil or military, without subscribing a declaration against transubstantiation; and as bullocks from Meath and Kildare brought down the price of fat stock in the English market, it declared the importation of cattle from Ireland to be "a public nuisance." In another session the business was clenched by an act prohibiting the introduction of these objectionable animals for ever; whether "dead or alive, great or small, fat or lean." Some members who objected were assured with the gracious courtesy reserved for Irish debates, that none "could oppose the bill but such as had Irish estates, or Irish understandings."

This was the reign of the "Merrie Monarch," a time of national enjoyment and revelry in England, interrupted only by an English Popish plot and massacre, more deliberate and bloody than the plot and massacre in Ulster, over which history is so clamorous. The plot was the famous invention of Titus Oates; the massacre was the trial, conviction and murder of his victims for eighteen months; whose execution went on merrily long after the time when judges and juries had ceased to believe a syllable of the evidence. These victims were English Catholics, because the inventors of the plot probably knew nothing personally of the Irish; but that Ireland had no share in a conspiracy to restore Popery, was so improbable that the patrons of the plot in London insisted on Irish victims. Oates and his comrades might make inconvenient blunders; but the Privy Council ordered the Lord Lieutenant to make proclamations for persons fit for the work. All who could make discoveries relating to Ireland were invited to come in without delay, and threatened with penalties if they were dilatory. There were at that time living in the country three men whom crime and want had made fit competitors with Dangerfield and Bedloe. They were living as cattle stealers and robbers, some of them liable to capital charges, but the character of witness of the plot was equal to a protection under the privy seal. One was a suspended priest, the others apostate friars, who had been expelled from their communities. These men charged Oliver Plunket, Primate of the Catholic Church, with having conspired to bring in a French expedition, and to levy an Irish army to aid them. His trial was ordered to be held in Dundalk; but as he was well known to the jurors, and the whole community there, no witnesses appeared when his arraignment took place. But this difficulty was promptly overcome; he was carried over to London, tried before an English jury, and on the ordinary incredible evidence of the period, convicted and executed. No man in England knew better than Charles Stuart, or admitted more frankly in private, that the plot was a fabrication, and its victims innocent men, but he was afraid to utter a word or perform an act to save them from murder. If the Catholic king who succeeded Charles had been strong and merciless as Cromwell, if he had slaughtered the judges, juries, and spectators of this massacre, and their contemporaries indiscriminately for the offence of being alive at the period, if he had sent Englishmen in thouands to be slaves in the West Indies, and women, to a worse fate, he would be qualified, doubtless, like Oliver, to be recognised as a benevolent agent of Divine justice.

When the death of Charles raised his brother to the throne James determined to establish religious liberty by suspending or annulling the penal laws against Catholics and Dissenters. It was a wise and just purpose, and if he had carried it out by the large influence of a king over the parliaments of that period, he would have had the applause of all good men. But he attempted to effect his purpose by royal prerogative and violated the Protestant constitution of the country. History has done slender justice to his memory, but Hallam an oracle on questions of constitutional law, declares of that period : "No man had been deprived of his liberty by any illegal warrant.

No man, except in the single instance of Magdalen College, had been despoiled of his property. The Government of James II. will lose little by comparison with that of his father; yet many, who scarcely put bounds to their eulogies of Charles I., have been content to abandon the cause of one who had no faults in his public conduct but such as seemed to come to him by inheritance."

James naturally sought support in Catholic Ireland which would have shared the benefit of his reform. The Irish never loved James, they knew him chiefly as a plantator in Tipperary, but his present offence was not such a one as could reasonably be expected to move their indignation. He was a Catholic and sought to extend religious liberty to Catholics and Dissenters. If his method was harsh and arbitrary, the boundaries of royal prerogative were ill-defined, and nations have never been slow to condone offences committed in their own interest. A little later the strictest Scottish Whigs forgave William for suspending statutes by his royal authority in Scotland; though suspending statutes by royal authority was the offence for which his predecessor had been driven from the throne. The laws in operation against the king's fellow Catholics, indeed, were such as a reasonable man could not justify, or a humane man endure. The religion of the State was guarded with more than Mahomedan rigour. It was a capital offence to receive a member of the dominant church into the Catholic fold. It was a capital offence for a member of the Society of Jesus to land on the soil of England. In the great Universities founded by Catholic piety no Catholic could hold an office. In the army which Catholic nobles had led to victory on so many memorable fields no Catholic noble could hold a commission; no Catholic peasant could carry a musket. To modify these barbarous laws was the clear duty of one having the authority and responsibility of a sovereign. If James had endured them without resistance he would have been known to posterity as the basest of the long line of English kings. But he undertook his appointed task in a perverse spirit. He was headstrong and arbitrary, and yet easily deluded. He counted on impunity because he believed the incredible doctrine preached from the pulpits of the English Church since the Restoration, that the duty of a subject was non-resistance, to the will of his prince in every extremity, and he determined to do by authority and force what he might have succeeded in effecting by persuasion and influence.

James selected as Lord Lieutenant in Ireland Richard Talbot, the head of an Anglo-Norman house which still remained Catholic, created him Duke of Tyrconnell, and gave him his confidence in a degree unusual to his frigid nature. Talbot is credited with a plentiful catalogue of vices by

English writers. It is probable that he was boastful and profligate, and perhaps unveracious, but he was certainly bold, resolute, and devoted to his master, and to the nation he was sent to rule. We must judge him by his age and his contemporaries. He was far from being so unscrupulous a partisan as Shaftesbury, the patron, if not the prompter, of Titus Oates, and he was a generous and chivalrous gentleman compared to the hero of Blenheim and Malplaquet. When a conspiracy to bring in the Prince of Orange began to be talked of, Talbot disarmed a large number of Protestant gentlemen, whom he suspected of sympathy with William, and armed and regimented the native population whom he knew to be friendly to James. What else indeed was an agent of James to do? The Protestant gentry were for the most part heirs of Cromwellian settlers, and hated James as a Papist, and feared him as a king who might call in question the title of their estates. They themselves had taken much stricter precautions; when they were in power, a Catholic was not permitted to possess the simplest weapon of defence; half-a-dozen Catholics meeting in Dublin or its neighbourhood constituted an illegal assembly, and in country districts Catholics were not allowed to leave their parish except to attend the neighbouring market. In periods of alarm the precaution has been taken by every Government in Ireland before and since; but so singular are the canons of criticism applicable to Irish affairs, that Lord Macaulay, who was a Cabinet Minister under Queen Victoria in 1848, when arms were taken from Munster Catholics and distributed among Ulster Orangemen, treats this precaution of Tyrconnell's as a grave and exceptional offence.

The principal employments, civil and military, in Ireland, were necessarily bestowed on native Catholics. "The highest offices of state, in the army, and in the Courts of Justice (groans Lord

Macaulay) were with scarcely an exception filled by Papists."* It was an intolerable grievance certainly, in a Catholic country, under a Catholic king, who had only a handful of Protestant partisans in the island, that Catholics were so employed. To be sure, in England when James's opponents got the upper hand, the highest offices of state, in the army, and in the courts, without a single exception, were filled with Protestants, but that was "*bien différent.*" While the Prince of Orange, in correspondence

* The new levies under Tyrconnell are described by Lord Macaulay as a terror to Protestant innkeepers; they swaggered into taprooms, drank freely, and probably paid irregularly, being but irregularly paid themselves. In truth they were no better or no worse than the ill-disciplined soldiers of that age, but the judicious reader will get a valuable light on the system on which Anglo-Irish history is written, if he notes that while no excuse can be found for the Irish recruits, English soldiers under identical circumstances are defended and justified. "The pay of the English and Danes (says the same writer,) was in arrears. They indemnified themselves by excesses and exactions for the want of what was their due, and it was hardly possible to punish them with severity for not choosing to starve with arms in their hands."

F

with some of James's privy councillors and generals, was collecting on the coast of Holland an army of Dutch, French, and German troops to invade his kingdom, the king summoned to his aid a portion of his army in Ireland, recruited like the army of his father in a large part from Irish Catholics. An army similarly recruited has since won memorable victories for England in Spain, Belgium, and France, in Africa, Asia and Australasia, but the proposal was received with a roar of indignation, and a deluge of libels. At the same time two Irish judges, one of them recognised even by unfriendly critics as the foremost man of his race, were sent to London to make certain representations respecting the condition of Ireland. These officials would have been received with distinction at Versailles or the Escuriel; in London the mob surrounded their carriage with burlesque ceremonies, among which potatoes stuck on white wands were conspicuous. The favourite jester of the present

INTRODUCTION. lxxxiii

day,* who ordinarily pictures an Irishman as a baboon or gorilla, is scarcely more delightfully humorous; and the perversity of a people who do not love such charming pleasantries, has naturally been the perplexity of English writers down to our own time.

While James was meditating a flight to France some good friend of the revolution indulged in a playful device of a more practical sort. A crowd of fugitives, whose dress bespoke them ploughmen and labourers, rushed into London at midnight, shrieking the dreadful news that the Irish army were in full march on the city, burning houses and slaughtering women and children in their course. Letters containing horrible versions of this Popish atrocity were delivered in distant and widely sundered districts of the country at the same time. The citizens rose and armed in self-defence, and as no enemy

* Mr. Punch.

appeared they passed the time agreeably in sacking and burning houses of Catholic gentlemen and tradesmen. The enemy never appeared, and the story turned out to be a pious fraud; a partisan of the Whigs afterwards claimed the merit of having schooled the shrieking fugitives with his own lips, and written the letters with his proper hand. The good bishop who saw the Protestant ghosts clamouring for an avenger in broad day light, on the bridge of Portadown, or the ingenious scribes who furnished the daily bulletins of the Massacre manufactured in London, scarcely deserved better of the State. Had he lived in our day he would probably have exercised his imagination in kindred pursuits and become an eminent historical critic.

James fled to France and left his enemies in possession of England and Scotland. In Ireland Tyrconnell held the country for the king, and sent him advice to head a French expedition to Dublin, where he would be loyally welcomed, and reinstated in a kingdom. Louis XIV. gave him officers, arms, ammunition and a little money, but no soldiers; and with this poor provision he landed at Kinsale in the spring of 1689. The Irish received him in triumph; installed him in Dublin Castle, the traditional seat of authority, and the best men of the race tendered him their service. A parliament was summoned. It necessarily consisted almost exclusively of Catholics. The Protestants elected amounted to about half a dozen. The Protestant peers who answered the king's summons reached about the same number, including three Protestant bishops; but small as the number was, it was certainly in excess of the proportion of Protestants in the country who supported James. And it was liberality and generosity compared to the practice it superseded. Up to the coming of James, and throughout a great part of the seventeenth century, an Irish Catholic found it as impossible to get elected to the legislature of his native country as an English Catholic has done in the nineteenth. There was but one Catholic in the Irish Parliament of Charles II. The Government was chiefly Catholic also, though James had several English Protestants in his Cabinet, but they were necessarily the minority. Lord Macaulay is disgusted at the number of O'Neills and O'Donovans, MacMahons and Macnamaras who thronged the benches of the Commons; a phenomenon as amazing as to see Russells and Stanleys, Smiths and Brownes, in the Parliament of Westminster. Other modern writers have made the scanty representation of the minority a subject of reproach. How the Irish Catholics could have been so bigoted as to prefer entrusting their interests to men of their own race and faith, is amazing to writers of a nation which two centuries later, out of five hundred and fifty representatives of England, Scotland and

Wales did not elect a single Catholic gentleman, and down to this day has never elected half a dozen to any one parliament.*

Such were the lessons of public morality and equal justice which the Irish people had received during the reigns of the ancestors of the exiled king of England, who threw himself upon their generosity. Their representatives in the new parliament, elected as soon as the king had taken up his abode in Dublin Castle, came to power without experience or discipline, because they had been basely excluded from the exercise of any public functions in their native country. If men with such antecedents had committed all the crimes attributed to them by dishonest writers, they would only have shown themselves apt pupils of English statesmen and sovereigns. But they had a few leaders of their

* Having formerly traversed the same period in a general survey of Irish History, I have reproduced the facts of the Stuart era from my "Bird's Eye View of Irish History" in "Young Ireland," re-published in a separate volume by James Duffy & Co., Dublin.

own race trained in France and England, into some acquaintance with public business, who discouraged all factious excesses, and the counsel of these leaders was loyally followed by the new parliament. There is scarcely in human history a more touching or impressive spectacle than the genuine fairness and moderation of this maligned parliament, and this is the story which is told in the following pages. I determined long ago to re-publish the narrative in some such collection as the present, a design confirmed by the judgment passed on Davis's work by so competent a critic as Mr. Lecky.* The scattered chapters

* "By far the best and fullest account of this Parliament with which I am acquainted is to be found in a series of papers upon it (which have unfortunately never been reprinted) by Thos. Davis, in the 'Dublin Magazine' of 1843. In these papers the Acts of Repeal and of Attainder are printed at length, and the extant evidence relating to them is collected and sifted with an industry and skill that leave little to be desired. I must take this opportunity of expressing my grateful thanks to Sir Gavan Duffy for having called my attention to these most valuable, but now almost forgotten papers."—Note on "Lecky's History of England in the Eighteenth Century." Vol. ii., p. 184.

INTRODUCTION. lxxxix

were originally printed from time to time in an obscure periodical, and fell dead from the press; but once they are known to students, it is not rash to predict that they will take their place permanently in historical as well as popular libraries.

C. GAVAN DUFFY.

Villa Guillory,
    Nice, *July*, 1893.

# THE AUTHOR'S PREFACE.

HIS enquiry is designed to rescue eminent men and worthy acts from calumnies which were founded on the ignorance and falsehoods of the Old Whigs, who never felt secure until they had destroyed the character as well as the liberty of Ireland.

Irish oppression never could rely on mere physical force for any length of time. Our enormous military resources, and the large proportion of "fighting men," or men who love fighting, among our people, prohibit it. It was ever necessary to divide us by circulating extravagant stories of our crimes and our disasters, in order to poison the wells of brotherly love and patriotism in our hearts, that so many of us might range ourselves under the banner of our oppressor.

Calumny lives chiefly on the past and future; it corrupts history and croaks dark prophecies. Never, from TYRCONNELL'S rally down to O'CONNELL'S revival of the Emancipation struggle—never, from the summons of the Dungannon Convention to the Corporation Debate on Repeal, has a single bold course been proposed for Ireland, that folly, disorder, and disgrace, has not been foreboded. Never has any great deed been done here that the alien Government did not, as soon as the facts became historical, endeavour to blacken the honour of the statesmen, the wisdom of the legislators, or the valour of the soldiers who achieved it.

One of the favourite texts of these apostles of misrule was the Irish Government in King JAMES'S time. "There's a specimen," they said, "of what an Irish Government would be—unruly, rash, rapacious, and bloody." But the King, Lords, and Commons of 1689, when looked at honestly present a sight to make us proud and hopeful for Ireland. Attached as they were to their King, their first act was for Ireland. They declared that the English Parliament had not, and never had, any right to legislate for Ireland, and that none, save the King and Parliament of Ireland, could make laws to bind Ireland.

In 1698, just nine years after, while the acts of this great Senate were fresh, MOLYNEUX published his case of Ireland, that case which SWIFT argued, and LUCAS urged, and FLOOD and GRATTAN, at the head of 70,000 Volunteers; carried, and England ratified against her will. Thus, then, the idea of 1782 is to be found full grown in 1689. The pedigree of our freedom is a century older than we thought, and Ireland has another Parliament to be proud of.

That Parliament, too, established religious equality. It anticipated more than 1782. The voluntary system had no supporters then, and that patriot Senate did the next best thing they left the tithes of the Protestant People to the Protestant Minister, and of the Catholic People to the Catholic Priest. Pensions not exceeding £200 a year, were given to the Catholic Bishops. And no Protestant Prelates were deprived of stipend or honour—they held their incomes, and they sat in the Parliament. They enforced perfect liberty of conscience; nor is there an act of theirs which could inform one ignorant of Irish faction to what creed the majority belonged. Thus for its moderation and charity this Parliament is an honour and an example to the country.

While on the one hand they restored the estates plundered by the Cromwellians thirty-six years before, and gave compensation to all innocent persons—while they strained every nerve to exclude the English from our trade, and to secure it to the Irish—while they introduced the Statute of Frauds, and many other sound laws, and thus showed their zeal for the peaceful and permanent welfare of the People, they were not unfit to grapple with the great military crisis. They voted large supplies; they endeavoured to make a war-navy; the leading members allowed nothing but their Parliamentary duties to interfere with their recruiting, arming, and training of troops. They were no timorous pedants, who shook and made homilies when sabres flashed and cannon roared. Our greatest soldiers, M'CARTHY and TYRCONNELL, and, indeed, most of the Colonels of the Irish regiments, sat in Lords or Commons;—not that the Crown brought in stipendiary soldiers, but that the Senate were fearless patriots, who were ready to fight as well as to plan for Ireland.

Theirs was no qualified preference for freedom if it were lightly won—they did not prefer

"Bondage with ease to strenuous liberty."

Let us then add 1689 to our memory; and when a Pantheon or Valhalla is piled up to commemorate the names and guard the effigies of the great and good, the bright and burning genius, the haughty and faithful hearts, and the victorious hands of Ireland, let not the men of that time—that time of glory and misfortune—that time of which Limerick's two sieges typify the clear and dark sides—defiance and defeat of the Saxon in one, trust on the Saxon and ruin in the other—let not the legislators or soldiers of that great epoch be forgotten.

THOMAS DAVIS.

*July* 1843.

# THE
# IRISH PARLIAMENT
## OF
# JAMES II.

## CHAPTER I.

A RETROSPECT.

How far the Parliament which sat in Dublin in 1689, was right or wrong, has been much disputed. As the history of it becomes more accurately and generally known, the grounds of this dispute will be cleared.

Nor is it of trifling interest to determine whether a parliament, which not only exercised great influence at the time, but furnished the enactors of the Penal Laws with excuses, and the achievers of the Revolution of

G

1782 with principles and a precedent, was the good or evil thing it has been called.

The writers commonly quoted against it are, Archbishop King, Harris, Leland; those in its favour, Leslie, Curry, Plowden, and Jones.* Of all these writers, King and Leslie are alone original authorities. Harris copies King, and Leland copies Harris, and Plowden, Curry, and Jones rely chiefly on Leslie. Neither Harris, Leland, nor Curry add anything to our knowledge of the time. King (notwithstanding, as we shall show hereafter, his disregard of truth) is valuable as a cotemporary of high rank; Leslie, also a cotemporary, and of unblemished character, is still more valuable. Plowden is a fair and sagacious commentator; Jones, a subtle and suggestive critic on those times.

If, in addition, the reader will consult such authorities as the Letters of Lord Lieutenant Tyrconnell;† the Memoirs‡ of James the Second by

---

* King's "State of the Protestants." Harris's "Life of King William," folio, Dublin, 1749, book 8. Leland's "History of Ireland," vol. 3, book 6, chaps. 5 and 6. Leslie's "Answer to King's State of the Protestants," London, 1692. Curry's "Review of the Civil Wars of Ireland." Plowden's "Historical Review of Ireland; also History of Ireland," vol. i., c. 9. Jones's "Reply to an anonymous writer from Belfast, signed Portia." Dublin, 1792.

† Thorpe's MSS.

‡ London, 2 vols. 4to edited by Rev. J. Clarke.

himself; *Histoire de la Révolution par Mazure;* \* and the pamphlets quoted in this publication, and the notes to it, he will be in a fair way towards mastering this difficult question.

After all, that Parliament must be judged by its own conduct: If its acts were unjust, bigotted, and rash, no excuse can save it from condemnation. If, on the other hand, it acted with firmness and loyalty towards its king,—if it did much to secure the rights, the prosperity, and the honour of the nation,—if, in a country where property had been turned upside down a few years before, it strove to do justice to the many, with the least possible injury to the few,—if, in a country torn with religious quarrels, it endeavoured to secure liberty of conscience without alienating the ultra zealous,—and finally, if in a country in imminent danger from a powerful invader and numerous traitors, it was more intent on raising resources and checking treason, than would become a parliament sitting in peace and safety, let us, while confessing its fallibility, attend to its difficulties, and do honour to its vigour and intelligence.

Before we mention the composition of the Parliament, it will be right to run over some of the chief dates and facts which brought about the state of things that led to its being summoned. Most Irishmen (ourselves among the number) are only beginners at Irish history, and cannot too often repeat the ele-

\* Paris, 1825, 3 vols. 8vo.

ments: still the beginning has been made. It is no pedantry which leads one to the English invasion, for the tap-root of the transactions of the seventeenth century.

Four hundred years of rapacious war and wild resistance had made each believe all things ill of the other; and when England changed her creed in the sixteenth century, it became certain that Ireland would adhere to hers at all risks. Accordingly, the reigns of the latter, and especially of the last of the Tudors, witnessed unceasing war, in which an appetite for conquest was inflamed by bigotry on the English side, while the native, who had been left unaided to defend his home, was now stimulated by foreign counsels, as well as by his own feelings, to guard his altar and his conscience too.

James the First found Ireland half conquered by the sword; he completed the work by treachery, and the fee of five-sixths of Ulster rewarded the "energy" of the British. The proceedings of Strafford added large districts in the other provinces to the English possessions. Still, in all these cases, as in the Munster settlement under Elizabeth, the bulk of the population remained on the soil. To leave the land was to die. They clung to it amid sufferings too shocking to dwell on;* they clung to it under such a serfhood as made the rapacity of their conquerors

---

* Spenser's "View"; Fynes Moryson's "Itinerary"; Captain Lee's "Memoir"; Harris's "Letters"; and Carte's "Ormonde."

interested in retaining them on the soil. They clung to it from necessity and from love. They multiplied on it with the rapidity of the reckless. Yet they retained hope, the hope of restitution and vengeance. The mad ferocity of Parsons and Borlace hastened the outbreak of 1641. That insurrection gave back to the native his property and his freedom, but compelled him to fight for it,—first, against the loyalists; next, against the traitors; and lastly, against the republicans. After a struggle of ten years, distinguished by the ability of the Council of Kilkenny, and the bravery of Owen Roe and his followers, the Irish sunk under the abilities and hosts of Cromwell. Those who felt his sway might well have envied the men who conquered and died in the breach of Clonmel, or fell vanquished or betrayed at Letterkenny and Drogheda. During the insurrection of 1641, the royal government, at once timid and tyrannical, united with the sordid capitalists of London to plunder the Irish of their lands and liberty, if not to exterminate them.\* In order to effect this, a system of unparalleled lying was set a-foot against the natives of this kingdom. The violence which naturally attended the sudden resumption of property by an ignorant, excited, and deeply wronged people, was magnified into a national propensity to throat-cutting. Exaggerations the most barefaced

\* See the proofs of this collected in Carey's "Vindiciæ Hibernicæ."

were received throughout England. Deaths, which the English-minded Protestant, the Rev. Mr. Warner, has ascertained to have been under 12,000, reckoning deaths from hardships along with those by the sword, —were rated in England at 150,000, and by John Milton at 616,000.* No wonder the English nation looked upon us as bloody savages; and no wonder they looked approvingly at the massacres and confiscations of the Lord Protector. But the Irish deemed they were free from crime, in resuming by force of arms the land which arms had taken from them; they regarded the bloodshed of '41 as a deplorable result of English oppression; they fought with the hearts of resolved patriots till 1651.

The restoration of the Stuarts was hailed as the restoration of their rights. They were woefully disappointed. A compromise was made between the legitimists and the republicans; the former were to resume their rank, the latter to retain their plunder. Ireland was disregarded. The mockery of the Court of Claims restored less than one-third of the Irish lands. While in 1641 the Roman Catholics possessed two-thirds of Ireland; in 1680, they had but one-fifth.† Besides, the new possessors were of an

* Milton's "Eikonoclastes"; Warner's "History of the Rebellion"; Carey's "Vindiciæ"; and Pamphlets, Libraries of Trinity College and the Dublin Society.

† Sir W. Petty's "Political Anatomy of Ireland"; Lawrence's "Interest of Ireland"; "Curry's Review", "Carte's Life and Letters of Ormonde," &c.

opposite creed, and fortified themselves by Penal Laws. Under such circumstances the aim of most men would be much the same, namely, to take the first opportunity of regaining their property, their national independence, and religious freedom. With reference to their legislation on the two latter points, doubts may be entertained how much should be complained of; and even those who condemn that on the first, should remember that "the re-adjustment of all private rights, after so entire a destruction of their landmarks, could only be effected by the coarse process of general rules."*

Let us now run over a few dates, till we come to the event which gave the Irish this opportunity. On the 6th of February, 1685, Charles the Second died in the secret profession of the Roman Catholic faith, and his brother, James Stuart, Duke of York, succeeded him.

James the Second came to his throne with much of what usually wins popular favour. He united in his person the blood of the Tudor, Plantagenet, and Saxon kings of England, while his Scottish descent came through every king of Scotland, and found its spring in the Irish Dalriad chief, who, embarking from Ulster, overran Albany. In addition, James had morals better than those of his rank and time, as much intellect as most kings, and the reputation

* Hallam's "Constitutional History," v. 3, p. 588, 3rd edition.

acquired from his naval administration, graced as it was by sea-fights in which no ship was earlier in action than James's, and by at least one great victory —that over Opdam—fought near Yarmouth, on the 3rd June, 1665.

Yet the difference of his creed from that of his English subjects blew these popular recollections to shivers. He tried to enforce, first—toleration; and secondly, perfect religious equality, and intended, as many thought, the destruction of that equality, by substituting a Roman Catholic for a Protestant supremacy; and the means he used for this purpose were such as the English Parliament had pronounced unconstitutional. He impeached the corporate charters by *quo warranto*, brought to trial before judges whom he influenced, as all his predecessors had done. He invaded the customs of the universities, as having a legal right to do so. He suspended the penal laws, and punished those who disobeyed his liberal but unpopular proclamations. Some noble zealots, the Russells and Sidneys, crossed his path in vain; but a few bold caballers, the Danbys, the Shaftesburys, and Churchills, by urging him to despotic acts, and the people to resistance, brought on a crisis; when, availing themselves of it, they called in a foreign army and drove out James, and swore he had abdicated; expelled the Prince of Wales, and falsely called him bastard; made terms with William, that he should have the crown and privy purse, and they the actual government; and ended by calling their selfish and hypocritical work, "a popular and glorious revolution."

It is needless to follow up James's quarrel with the university of Oxford, and his unsuccessful prosecution of the seven Bishops on the 29th of June, 1688, who, emboldened by the prospect of a revolution, refused to read his proclamation of indulgence. From the day of their acquittal, James was lost. Letters were circulated throughout England* and Ireland, declaring the young Prince of Wales (who was born 10th June) spurious, and containing many other falsehoods, so as to shake men's souls with rumours, and arouse popular prejudices. The army was tampered with; the nobles and clergy were in treaty with Holland. James not only refused to retract his policy till it was too late; but refused, too, the offer of Louis to send him French troops.

Similar means had been used by and against him in Ireland. Tyrconnell, who had replaced Clarendon as Lord Lieutenant in 1686, got in the charters of the corporations; reconstructed the army, and used every means of giving the Roman Catholics that share in the government of this country, to which their numbers entitled them. And on the other hand, the Protestant nobles joined the English conspiracy, and adopted the English plan of false plots and forged letters.

* Speke's "Memoirs."

At length, on 4th November, 1688, Prince William landed at Torbay with 15,000 veterans. James attempted to bear up, but his nearest and dearest, his relatives and his favourites, deserted him in the hour of his need. It seems not excessive to say, that there never was a revolution in which so much ingratitude, selfishness, and meanness were displayed. There is not one great genius or untainted character eminent in it. Yet it succeeded. On the 18th of December, William entered London ; on the 23rd, James sailed for France; and in the February following, the English convention declared he had *abdicated.*

These dates are, as Plowden remarks, important ; for though James's flight, on the 23rd of December, was the legal pretence for insurrection in the summer of 1689, yet negociations had been going on with Holland through 1687 and 1688,* and the Northern Irish formed themselves into military corps, and attacked the soldiers of the crown before Inniskillen, on the *first week* in December; and on the 7th December the gates of Derry were shut in the face of the king's troops,† facts which should be remembered in judging the loyalty of the two parties.

---

*See the Declaration of Union, dated 21st March, 1688 in the Appendix to Walker's " Account of the Siege of Derry."

† These acts were done in good faith by the people, instigated by the devices of the nobles. A letter, now admitted to have been forged, was dispersed by Lord Mount Alexander, announcing the design of the Roman Catholics to murder the Protestants.

## CHAPTER II.
ORIGIN AND CHARACTER OF THE PARLIAMENT.—THE HOUSE OF LORDS.

JAMES landed at Kinsale, 12th March, 1689, about a month after the election of William and Mary by the English convention. He entered Dublin in state on the 24th March, accompanied by D'Avaux, as Ambassador from France, and a splendid court. His first act was to issue five proclamations,—the first, requiring the return and aid of his Irish absentee subjects; the second, urging upon the local authorities the suppression of robberies and violence which had increased in this unsettled state of affairs; the third, encouraging the bringing provisions for his army; the fourth, creating a currency of such metal as he had, conceiving it preferable to a paper currency (a gold or silver currency was out of his power, for of the two millions promised him by France, he only got £150,000); the fifth proclamation summoned a parliament for the 7th May, 1689.

James also issued a proclamation promising liberty of conscience, justice and protection\* to all; and, after

\* See as to this, Melfort's letter to Pottinger, the sovereign of Belfast; "History of Belfast," pp. 72-3: Lesley *proves*, on Williamite authority, that the Protestants were worse treated by William's army than by James's. See Dr. Gorges in Lesley's Appendix.

receiving many congratulatory addresses, set out for Derry to press the blockade. On the 29th April, he returned to Dublin. On the 7th May, Ireland possessed a complete and independent government. Leaving the castle, over which floated the national flag, James proceeded in full procession to the King's Inns, where the Parliament sat, and the Commons having assembled at the bar of the Peers, James entered, "with Robe and Crown," and addressed the Commons in a speech full of manliness and dignity. At the close of the speech the Chancellor of Ireland, Lord Gosworth, directed the Commons to retire and make choice of a Speaker. In half an hour the Commons returned and presented Sir Richard Nagle as their Speaker, a man of great endowments and high character. The Speaker was accepted, and the Houses adjourned.

The peers who sat in this parliament amounted to fifty-four. Among these fifty-four, were six dignitaries of the Protestant church, one duke, ten earls, sixteen viscounts, and twenty-one barons. It contained the oldest families of the country,—O'Brien and DeCourcy, MacCarty and Bermingham, De Burgo and Maguire, Butler and Fitzpatrick. The bishops of Meath, Cork, Ossory, Limerick, and Waterford, and the Protestant names of Aungier, Le Poer, and Forbes sat with the representatives of the great Roman Catholic houses of Plunket, Barnewell, Dillon, and Nugent. Nor were some fresher honours wanting; Talbot and

Mountcashel were the darlings of the people, the trust of the soldiery, the themes of bards.

King's impeachment of this parliament is amusing enough. His first charge is, that if the House were full, the majority would have been Protestant. Now if the majority preferred acting as insurgents under the Prince of Orange, to attending to their duties in the Irish house of peers, it was their own fault. Certain it is, the most violent might safely have attended, for the earls of Granard and Longford, and the bishop of Meath not only attended, but carried on a bold and systematic opposition. And so far was the House from resenting this, that they committed the sheriff of Dublin to prison, for billeting an officer at the bishop of Meath's. Yet the bishop had not merely resisted their favourite repeal of the Settlement, but, in doing so, had stigmatized their fathers and some of themselves as murderous rebels.

King's next charge is, that the attainders of many peers were reversed to admit them. Now this is unsupported by evidence, against fact, and simply a falsehood. Then he complains of the new creations. They were just *five* in number ; and of these five, two were great legal dignitaries—the Lord Chancellor and Lord Chief Justice of Ireland ; the third was Col. MacCarty of the princely family of Desmond, and a distinguished soldier with a great following—the others, Brown, Lord Kenmare ; and Bourke, Lord Bofin (son of Lord Clanricarde), men of high position in their counties.

Fitton, Lord Gosworth, occupied the woolsack. That he was a man of capacity if not of character, may be fairly presumed from his party having put him in so important an office in such trying times.* He certainly had neither faction nor following to bring with him. Nor was he treated by his party below what his rank entitled him to. The appointments in his court were not interfered with: his decrees were not impeached, and in the council he sat above even Herbert the Lord Chancellor of England. Yet, King describes this man as " detected of forgery," one who was brought from gaol to the woolsack—one who had not appeared in any court—a stranger to the kingdom, the laws and the practice and rules of court;—one who made constant needless references to the Masters to disguise his ignorance, and who was brought into power, first, because he was " a convert papist, that is, a renegade to his country and his religion;" and secondly, because he would enable the Irish to recover their estates by countenancing " forgeries and perjuries," which last, continues the veracious archbishop, he nearly effected, without putting them to the trouble of repealing the Acts of Settlement. King staggers from the assertion that Fitton denied justice to Protestants, into saying it was got from him with difficulty.

Thomas Nugent, Baron Riverstown, second son of the Earl of Westmeath, was chosen chairman of committees. King, who is the only authority at present

* He was appointed in 1686 (see Appendix B). T. W. R.

accessible to us, states that Nugent had been "out" in 1641, but considering that he did not die till 1715, he must have been a mere boy in '41, if born at all; and, at any rate, as his family, including his grandfather Lord Delvin (first Earl Westmeath) and his father, carried arms against the Irish up to 1648, and suffered severely, it is most improbable that he was, as a child, in the opposite ranks.

The Irish had never ceased to agitate against the Acts of Settlement and Explanation. Thus Sir Nicholas Plunket had done legal battle against the first, till an express resolution excluded him by name from appearing at the bar of the council. Then Col. Talbot (Tyrconnell) led the opposition effort for their repeal or mild administration. In 1686, Sir Richard Nagle went to England, as agent of the Irish, to seek their repeal. But the greatest effort was made in 1688. Nugent and Rice were sent expressly to London to press the repeal. Rice is said to have shown great tact and eloquence, but Nugent to have been rash and confused. Certain it is, they were unsuccessful with the council, and were brutally insulted by the London mob, set on by the very decent chiefs of the Williamite party.

Of the eighteen prelates, ten were Englishmen, one Welsh, and only seven Irish. Several had been chaplains to the different lords lieutenant. Eleven out of the eighteen were in England during the session. Of these, some were habitual absentees, such as

Thomas Hackett, bishop of Down, deprived in 1691 by Williamite commissioners, for an absence of twenty years. Others had got leave of absence during '87 and '88. Some, like Archbishop John Vesey of Tuam, and Bishop Richard Tennison of Killala, fled in good earnest, and accepted lectureships and cures in London.

There was one man among them who deserves more notice, Anthony Dopping, lord bishop of Meath. He was born in Dublin 28th March, 1643, and died 24th April, 1697. He was educated in St. Patrick's schools, and won his fellowship in T. C. D. in 1662, being only 19 years old. He led the opposition in the parliament of '89 with great vigor and pertinacity. He resisted all the principal measures, and procured great changes in some of them, as appears by "The Journal." He had a fearless character and ready tongue. He continued a leader of the Ultras after the battle of the Boyne, and quarrelled with the government. King William, finding how slowly the Irish war proceeded, had prepared and sent to Ireland a proclamation conceding the demands of the Roman Catholics, granting them perfect religious liberty, right of admission to all offices, and an establishment for their clergy.* While this was with the printers in

---

* In July, 1691, William had offered these terms: 1st. The free public exercise of the Roman Catholic religion : 2nd. Half the churches in the kingdom : 3rd. Half the employments, civil and military, if they pleased : 4th. Half their properties, as

Dublin, news came of the danger of Limerick. The proclamation was suppressed by the Lords Justices, who hastened to the camp, "to hold the Irish to as hard terms as possible. This they did effectually." Still these "hard terms" were too lenient for the Ultras, who roared against the treaty of Limerick, and demanded its abrogation. On the Sunday after the Lords Justices had returned, full of joy at having tricked the Irish into so much harder terms than William had directed them to offer, they attended Christ Church, and the bishop of Meath preached a sermon, whose whole object was to urge the breaking of the treaty of Limerick, contending (says Harris, in his Irish Writers in Ware, p. 215) that "peace ought not to be kept with a people so perfidious." The Justices, and the Williamite or moderate party, were enraged at this. The bishop of Kildare was directed to preach in Christ Church on the following Sunday, in favour of the treaty; and he obtained the place in the privy council from which the bishop of Meath was expelled: but ultimately the party of the latter triumphed, and enacted the penal laws.

The list of the Lords Temporal has been made out with great care, from all the authorities accessible.

Ireland had then but two dukes, Tyrconnell and Ormond. Ormond possessed the enormous spoils

held prior to Cromwell's conquest. The terms were at once refused. The suppressed proclamation doubtless offered at least as much. (Harris's "William," and Plowden, b. 2.)

acquired by his grandfather from the Irish, and was therefore largely interested in the success of the English party. He of course did not attend. His huge territory and its regal privileges were taken from him by a special act.

Considering the position he occupied, the materials on the life of Tyrconnell are most unsatisfactory. Richard Talbot was a cadet of the Irish branch of the Shrewsbury family, and numbered in his ancestors the first names in English history. His father was Sir William Talbot, a distinguished Irish lawyer, and his brother, Peter Talbot, was R. C. archbishop of Dublin, and was murdered there by tedious imprisonment on a false charge in 1680. He was a lad of sixteen when Cromwell sacked Drogheda in September, 1649, and he doubtless brought from its bloody ashes no feeling in favour of the Saxon. He was all his life engaged in the service of the Irish and of James. He was attached to the Duke of York's suite from the Restoration, and was taken prisoner by the Dutch, on board the Catharine, in the naval action at Solebay, 29th May, 1672.* After the Acts of Settlement and Explanation were passed, he acted as agent for the Irish Roman Catholics, urging their claims with all the influence his rank, abilities, and fortune† could

---

*Rawdon Papers, p. 253.
†Anthony Hamilton, in his "Memoirs of Grammont," exaggerates this to £40,000 a year, and attributes Miss Jennings' affection to its attractions. But beside that, by his statement, Tyrconnell

command. His zeal got him into frequent dangers; he was sent to the Tower in 1661 and 1671, for having challenged the Duke of Ormond, and the English Commons presented an address in 1671, praying his dismissal from all public employments. He was selected by James, both from personal trust and popularity, to communicate with the Irish; and though Clarendon was first sent as Lord Lieutenant in '85, Tyrconnell had the independent management of the army,* and replaced Clarendon in 1686.

Sarsfield, who was at the head of "the French party," and most of the great Irish officers, thought him undecided, hardly bold enough, and with a selfish leaning towards England. Of his selfishness we have now a better proof than they had, a proof that *might* have abated his master's eulogy, given further on. We say *might*, for *possibly* Tyrconnell was in communication with James as to the French offers.

had been a rival of Grammont with Miss Hamilton, there is enough in Grammont to account for it otherwise. Hamilton, an Irishman and a Jacobite, seems to have sympathised with Tyrconnell. He describes him as "one of the largest and most powerful looking men in England," "with a brilliant and handsome appearance, and something of nobility, not to say haughtiness in his manners." He mentions circumstances, showing him bold, free, amorous, and, strange for a courtier, punctual in payment of debts. Yet this man, so full of refinement, and so trained, is described by King as addressing the Irish Privy Council thus:— "I have put the sword into your hands, and God damn you all if ever you part with it."

*Clarendon's " State Letters," vol. i. and the Diary.

"It is now ascertained that, doubtful of the king's success in the struggle for restoring popery in England, he had made secret overtures to some of the French agents, for casting off all connection with that kingdom in case of James's death, and, with the aid of Louis placing the crown of Ireland on his own head. M. Mazure has brought this remarkable fact to light. Bonrepos, a French emissary in England, was authorised by his court to proceed in a negociation with Tyrconnell for the separation of the two islands, in case that a Protestant should succeed to the crown of England. He had accordingly a private interview with a confidential agent of the lord lieutenant at Chester, in the month of October, 1687. Tyrconnell undertook that in less than a year everything should be prepared."\*

Tyrconnell was made Baron Talbotstown, Viscount Baltinglass, and Earl of Tyrconnell in 1686, and Duke and Marquis, 30th March, 1689.

From his coming to Ireland, he worked hard for his master and his countrymen. He gradually substituted Jacobite soldiers for the Oliverians, who till then filled the ranks. He increased the army largely, and lent the king 3,000 men in '88. Mischief was done to James's cause by this employment of Irish troops in England. He was active in calling in the corporation charters, and was exposed to much calumny on account of it. The means, doubtless, were indefensible, (for the change should have been effected by act of Parliament, as it has at length been in our times,) but the end was to put the corporations into the hands of the

---

\* Hallam's "Constitutional History," v. iii., p. 530.

Irish people. And even in those new corporations, one-third of the burgesses were of English descent and Protestant faith; but this moderation is attempted to be shaved away by the Williamites, who insist that most of these Protestants were Quakers, whom they describe as a savage rabble, originally founded by the Jesuits\* —with what injustice we need hardly say. James describes him "as a man of good abilities and clear courage, and one who for many years had a true attachment to his majesty's person and interest."†

Lord Clanrickarde represented the Mac William *Uachdar*, one of the two great branches of the De Burgos, who usurped the chieftainry on the death of the Earl of Ulster in the year 1333. His father was the great Lord Clanrickarde, who held Connaught in peace and loyalty, from 1641 to 1650; when the troops for which he had negociated with the Duke of Lorraine not arriving, he too yielded to the storm.

Mac Donnel Lord Antrim, also the representative of a great house (the Lords of the Isles) was equally dependant on his predecessor for notoriety. His elder

---

\* State Tracts, Will. III.'s reign, II. R.'s App. to Cox.

† " Memoirs of James II." by the Rev. — Clarke, chaplain to George IV. These memoirs seem to have been copies of memoirs written under James II.'s inspection, and deposited in the Scotch College in Paris. The originals perished at the French Revolution, and their copies came to Rome, from whence they were procured for the English government in 1805. See Mr. Clarke's preface, and Guizot's preface to his translation of them in the " Mémoires de la Révolution."

brother, the Marquis and Earl of Antrim, played a notorious and powerful part on the Irish side, in the war, from 1642 up to 1650. This Earl Alexander also commanded an Irish regiment during the same war. He was within the treaty of Limerick, and saved his rank and fortune.

Lords Longford and Granard were Williamites in fact. This does not follow from their having acted so vigorously in the opposition in 1689, but from their having joined William openly the year after. Lord Granard had been offered the command of the Williamites of Ulster in 1688, and on his refusal, Lord Mount Alexander was appointed.

Among the earls, one naturally looks for the two famous names of Taaffe and Lucan. But Taaffe was then on an embassy to the emperor, and Patrick Sarsfield was not made Earl of Lucan till after. Indeed his patent is not entered in the rolls, from which 'tis probable he was not titled till after the battle of the Boyne.

Viscount Iveagh held Drogheda at the battle of the Boyne, and was induced to surrender it by William's ruffianly and unmilitary threat of "no quarter."

Lord Clare was father to the famous Lord Clare, whose regiment was the glory of the Irish Brigade, and who was killed at Ramillies in 1706. He was descended from Connor O'Brian, third earl of Thomond.

Lord Mountcashel, by his rapidity and skill,

completely broke the Munster insurgents, and made that province, till then considered the stronghold of the English, James's best help. To him was intrusted the Bill repealing the Settlement in the Commons, where he sate as member for the county of Cork till that Bill passed the Commons, when he was called to the Upper House as Lord Mountcashel.

Lord Kinsale represented the famous John De Courcy, Earl of Ulster, and had the blood of Charlemagne in his veins. He served as Lieutenant-Colonel to Lord Lucan. His attainder under William was reversed, and he appeared at court, where he enforced the privilege peculiar to his family, of remaining covered in the king's presence.

## CHAPTER III.

#### THE HOUSE OF COMMONS.

THE number of members in the Commons, as the complement was made up under the monstrous charters of James I., Charles I., and Charles II., far outdoing in their unconstitutional nature, any of the stretchings of prerogative in the reign of James II., amounted to 300. The number actually returned was 224. Of the deficiencies, no less than 28 were caused by the places being the seats of the war.

The character of this assembly must be chiefly judged by its acts, and we shall presently resume the consideration of them; but there are some things in the composition of the Commons whereby their character has been judged.

They have been denounced by King: but before we examine his statements, let us inquire who he was, lest we underrate or overrate his testimony; lest we unjustly require proof, in addition to the witness of a thoroughly pure and wise man; or, what is more dangerous, lest we remain content with the unconfirmed statements of a bigot or knave.

William King was the son of James King, a miller,

who, in order to avoid taking the Solemn League and Covenant, removed from the North of Scotland, and settled in Antrim, where William was born, 1st of May, 1650. (See Harris's "Ware," Bishops of Derry.) He was educated at Dungannon, was a sizar, "*native*," and schoolmaster in T.C.D., and was ordained in 1673. Parker, archbishop of Tuam, gave him a heap of livings, and on being translated to Dublin, procured the Chancellorship of St. Patrick's for King in 1679. This he held during the Revolution. He was imprisoned in 1689 on suspicion, but after some months was released, through the influence of Herbert and Tyrconnell, and notwithstanding C. J. Nugent's opposition. Immediately on his release, he wrote his "State of the Protestants of Ireland," printed in London, *cum privilegio*, at the chief Williamite printer's. It was written and published while the war in Ireland was at its height, and when it was sought at any price to check the Jacobite feeling then beginning to revive in England, by running down the conduct of the Irish, James's most formidable supporters. Moreover, King had been imprisoned, (justly or unjustly) by James's council, and he obtained the bishopric of Derry from William, on the 25th of January, 1690 (old style) namely, within thirty-eight weeks before the publication of his book, which was printed, *cum privilegio*, 15th of October, 1691. Whether the bishopric was the wages of the book, or the book revenge for the imprisonment, we shall not say; but surely King must have had marvellous virtue to write impartially, in excited and reckless times, for so demoralized a party as the English Whigs, when he wrote of transactions yet incomplete, of which there was a perilous stake not only for him but for his friends, and when, of the parties at issue, one gave him a gaol and the other a mitre.

There is scarcely a section in his book that does not abound with the most superlative charges, put in the coarsest language. All the calumnies as to 1641, which are now confessed to be false, are gospel truths in his book. He never gives an exact authority for any of his graver charges, and his appendix is a valuable reply to his text.

When, in addition to these external probabilities and intrinsic evidences of falsehood, we add that, immediately on its publication, Lesley wrote an answer to it, denying its main statements as mere lies, and that his book was never replied to, we will not be in a hurry to adopt any statement of King's.

But in order to see the force of this last objection to King's credibility, something must be known of Lesley.

Charles Lesley, son of the bishop of Clogher, is chiefly known for his very able controversial writings against Deists, Catholics, and Dissenters. He was a law-student till 1680, when he took orders; and in 1687 became chancellor of Connor. When, in 1688, James appointed a Roman Catholic sheriff for Monaghan,

Mr. Lesley being then sick with gout, had himself carried to the court-house, and induced the magistrates to commit the sheriff. In fact, it appears from Harris ("Life of William," p. 216 and "Writers of Ireland," pp. 282-6), that Lesley was notorious for his conversions of Roman Catholics, and his stern hostility to Tyrconnell's government. Lesley refused to take the oath of supremacy after the Revolution, and thereby lost all chance of promotion in the Church. He was looked on as the head of the nonjurors, and died in March, 1721-2, at Glaslough, universally respected.

Such being Mr. Lesley's character, so able, so upright, so zealously Protestant, he, in 1692, wrote an answer to King's "State," in which he accuses King of the basest personal hypocrisy, and charges him with having in his book written gross, abominable and notorious falsehoods, and this he *proves* in several instances, and in many more, renders it highly probable. King died 8th May, 1729, leaving Lesley's book altogether unreplied to.

Here then was that man—bishop of Derry for eleven years and archbishop of Dublin for twenty-seven years—remaining silent under a charge of deliberate and interested falsehood, and that charge made by no unworthy man, but by one of his own country, neighbourhood, and creed—by one of acknowledged virtue, high position, and vast abilities.

Nor is this all; Lesley's book was not only unanswered; it was watched and attempted to be stopped, and when published was instantly ordered to be suppressed, as were all other publications in favour of the Irish or of King James.

The reader is now in a position to judge of the credibility of any assertion of King's, when unsupported by other authority.

King's gravest charges are in the following passage :—

"These members of the House of Commons are elected either by freeholders of counties, or the freemen of the corporations; and I have already showed how king James wrested these out of the hands of Protestants, and put them into Popish hands in the new constitution of corporations, by which the freemen and freeholders of cities or boroughs, to whom the election of burgesses originally belongs, are excluded, and the election put into the hands of a small number of men named by the king, and removeable at his pleasure. The Protestant freeholders, if they had been in the kingdom, were much more than the papist freeholders, but now being gone, though many counties could not make a jury, as appeared at the intended trial of Mr. Price and other Protestants at Wicklow, who could not be tried for want of freeholders,—yet, notwithstanding the paucity of these, they made a shift to return knights of the shire. The common way of election was thus :—The Earl of Tyrconnell, together with the writ for election, commonly sent a letter, recommending the persons he designed should be chosen; the sheriff or mayor being his creature, on receipt of this, called so many of the freeholders of a county, or burgesses of a corporation together, as he thought fit, and without making any noise, made the return. It was easie to do this in boroughs—because, by their new charters, the electors were not above twelve or thirteen, and in the greatest cities but twenty-four; and commonly, not half of these in the place. The method of the sheriff's proceeding was the same; the number of Popish freeholders being very small, sometimes not a dozen in a county, it was easie to give notice to them to appear, so that the Protestants either did not know of the election, or durst not appear at it."

First let us see about the boroughs. King, in his section on the corporations, states in terms that "they" (the Protestants) "thought it reasonable to keep these (corporate towns) in their own hands, as being the foundation of the legislative power, and therefore secluded papists, &c." The purport therefore of King's objection to the new constitution under King James's charters, was the admission of Roman Catholics. Religious equality was sinful in his eyes.

The means used by James to change the corporations, namely, bringing *quo warrantos* in the Exchequer against them, and employing all the niceties of a confused law to quash them, we have before condemned. In doing so, he had the precedents of the reigns called most constitutional by English historians, and those not old, but during his brother's reign; nor can anyone who has looked into Brady's treatise on Boroughs, doubt that there was plenty of "law" in favour of James's conduct.* But still public policy and public opinion in England were against these *quo warrantos*,

---

* Hallam ("Constitutional History," caps. 13 and 14) contains enough to show the uncertainty of the law. Throughout these, as in all parts of his work, he is a zealous Williamite and a bigoted Whig. His treatment of Curry has been justly censured by Mr. Wyse, in his valuable "History of the Catholic Association," vol. i., pp. 36-7.

and in Ireland they were only approved of by those who were to be benefited by them.

But the means being thus improper, the use made by James of this power can hardly be complained of. The Roman Catholics were then about 900,000, the Protestants over 300,000. James, it is confessed, allowed one-third of the corporations to be Protestant, though they were little, if at all more than one-fourth of the population. This will appear no great injustice in our times, although some of these Protestants may, as it has been alleged, have been "Quakers."

It must also be remembered, that those proceedings were begun not by James but by Charles; that the corporations were, with some show of law, conceived to have been forfeited during the Irish war, or the Cromwellian rule; and that being offered renewals on terms, they refused; whereupon the *quo warrantos* were brought and decided before the regular tribunals, during the earlier and middle part of James's reign. On the 24th September, 1687, James issued his Royal Letter (to be found in Harris's Appendix, pp. 4 to 6), commanding the renewal of the charters. By these renewals, the first members of the corporations were to be named by the lord lieutenant, but they were afterwards to be elected by the corporations themselves. There certainly are *non-obstante* and non-resistance clauses ordered to be inserted, in the prerogative spirit of that day, which were justly complained of.

With reference to the number of burgesses, King's

statement that the number of electors was usually twelve or thirteen, and in the greatest cities but twenty-four, is untrue. Most of the Irish boroughs were certainly reduced to these numbers under the liberal Hanoverian government, but not so under James. The members' names are given in full in Harris's Appendix, and from those it appears that no corporation had so few as twelve electors. Only five, viz.— Dungannon, Ennis, St. Johnstown (in Longford), Belturbet, and Athboy, were as low as thirteen; twenty-three, viz.—Tuam, Kildare, Cavan, Galway, Callan, Newborough, Carlingford, Gowran, Carysfort, Boyle, Roscommon, Athy, Strabane, Middletown, Newry, Philipstown, Banagher, Castlebar, Fethard, Blessington, Charleville, Thomastown, and Baltimore varied from fourteen to twenty-four; most of the rest varied from thirty to forty. Dublin had seventy-three, Cork, sixty-one, Clonmel, forty-six, Cashel, forty-two, Drogheda, fifty-seven, Kilkenny, sixty-one, Limerick, sixty-five, Waterford, forty-nine, Youghal, forty-six, Wexford, fifty-three, and Derry, sixty-four. This is a striking proof of the little reliance to be placed on King's positive statements.

Harris, a hostile authority, gives the names, and generally the additions of the members of each corporation, and the majority are merchants, respectable traders, engineers, or gentlemen. Moreover, in such towns as our local knowledge extends to, the names are those of the best families, not being zealous

Williamites. As to the counties, King relies upon a pamphlet published in London in 1689, setting out great grievances in the title page, and disproving them in the body of the tract.

If many Protestant freeholders had fled to England, who was to blame?—Most assuredly, my Lord Mount Alexander and the rest of the right noble and honourable suborners, devisers, and propagators of forged letters and infamous reports, whereby they frightened the Protestants, in order to take advantage of their terror for their own selfish ends. The exposure of these devices by the publication of "Speke's Memoirs," by the confessed forgery of the Dromore letter, &c., have thrown the chief blame of the Protestant desertion off the shoulders of those Protestants, off the shoulders, too, of the Irish government, and have brought it crushingly upon the aristocratic cabal, who alone profited by the revolution, as they alone caused it.

In the absence of other testimony, we must take, with similar allowances, the story of Tyrconnell "*commonly*" sending an unconstitutional letter to influence the election. But how very good these Jacobite sheriffs and mayors were, to let King into the secret, in 1691, when their destiny was uncertain! That such gossip was current is likely, but for a historian to assert on such authority is scandalous.

King asserts that the unrepresented boroughs were "*about twenty-nine.*" Now, there were but *eighteen* boroughs unrestored; but King helps out the falsehood by inserting places—Thurles, Tipperary, Arklow, and Birr—which *never* had members before or since, by *creating* a *second* town of Kells, by transferring St. Johnstown in Longford, which returned members, to St. Johnstown in Donegal, which was a seat of war, and by other tricks equally discreditable to his honesty and intelligence.

The towns unrestored *could* not have sent members to James's parliament, and it was apparently doubted whether they ought to have done so to William's in '92.

Against the Commons actually elected, the charge is, that only six Protestants were elected. In the very section containing the charge, it is much qualified by other statements. "Thus," he says, "one Gerard Dillon, Sergeant-at-Law, a most furious Papist, was Recorder of Dublin, and he stood to be chosen one of the burgesses for the city, but could not prevail, because he had purchased a considerable estate under the Act of Settlement, and they feared lest this might engage him to defend it;" and therefore they chose Sir Michael Creagh and Terence Dermot, their Senior Aldermen, showing pretty clearly that the good citizens of Dublin set little value on the "furious Popery" of Prime Sergeant Dillon, in comparison with their property plundered by the Act of Settlement.

The election for Trinity College is worthy of notice. We have it set out in flaming paragraphs how horribly the College was used, worse than any other borough,

"Popish Fellows" being intruded. "In the house they placed a Popish garrison, turned the chapel into a magazine, and many of the chambers into prisons for Protestants." (King, p. 220, Ed. 1744.) Yet, *miraculous* to say, in the heart of this "Popish garrison," the "turned-out Vice-Provost, Fellows, and Scholars" met, and elected two most bold, notable, and Protestant Williamites.

If this election could take place in Dublin, under the very nose of the Government, and in a corporation in which the king had unquestioned control, one will hesitate about the compulsion or exclusion in other places.

Besides, Sir John Meade and Mr. Joseph Coghlan, the members for the College, there "were four more Protestants returned, of whose behaviour I can give no account," says King. Pity he does not give the names.

If we were to allow a similar error in King's account of the creed of the elected, that we have proved in his lists of the borough electors, it would raise the number of Protestants in the house to about fourteen.

Allowing then for the Protestants in arms against the Government—out of the country,—or within the seat of war—the disproportion between their representatives and the Roman Catholics will lessen greatly.

One thing more is worth noticing in the Commons, and that is a sort of sept representation. Thus we see

O'Neills in Antrim, Tyrone, and Armagh; Magennises in Down, O'Reillys in Cavan; Martins, Blakes, Kirwans, Dalys, Bourkes, for Connaught; MacCarthys, O'Briens, O'Donovans for Cork and Clare; Farrells for Longford; Graces, Purcells, Butlers, Welshs, Fitzgeralds, for Tipperary, Kilkenny, Kildare, &c.; O'Tooles, Byrnes, and Eustaces for Wicklow; MacMahons for Monaghan; Nugents, Bellews, Talbots, &c., for North Leinster.

Sir Richard Nagle, the Speaker, was the descendant of an old Norman family (said to be the same as the Nangles) settled in Cork. His paternal castle, Carrignancurra, is on the edge of a steep rock, over the meadows of the Blackwater, half-a-dozen miles below Mallow. It is now the property of the Foot family, and here may still be seen the mouldering ruin where that subtle lawyer first learned to plan. Peacefully now look the long oak-clad cliffs on the happy river.

Nagle had obtained a splendid reputation at the Irish Bar. "He had been educated among the Jesuits, and designed for a clergyman," says King, "but afterwards betook himself to the study of the law, in which he arrived to a good perfection." Harris, likewise, calls him "an artful lawyer of great parts." Tyrconnell valued him rightly, and brought him to England with him in the autumn of 1686. His reputation seems to have been great, for it seems the lords interested in the Settlement Act, "on being informed of Nagle's arrival, were so transported with rage, that they would have had him immediately sent out of London."

He was knighted and made attorney-general in 1687; and on James's arrival, March, 1688-9, he was made secretary of state. He is said, we know not how truly, to have drafted the Commons' bill for the repeal of the Settlement.

Let us mention some of the members.—Nagle's colleague in Cork was Colonel MacCarty, afterwards Lord Mountcashel. Miles de Courcy, afterwards Lord Kinsale. MacCarty Reagh who finally settled in France. His descendant Count MacCarty Reagh, was notable for having one of the finest libraries in Europe, which was sold after the Revolution.

The Rt. Hon. Simon Lutteral raised a dragoon regiment for James, and afterwards commanded the Queen's regiment of infantry in the Brigade. He was father to Colonel Henry Lutteral, accused of having betrayed the passage of the Shannon at Limerick; and though Harris throws doubt on this particular act of treason, his correspondence and rewards from William seem sufficient proof and confirmation of his guilt.

Lally of Tullendaly, member for Tuam, was the representative of the O'Lallys an old Irish sept. His brother John Gerard Lally settled in France, and married a sister to Dillon, *" colonel propriétaire"* in the Brigade, and was Colonel commanding in this illustrious regiment

Sir Gerard was father to the famous Count Thomas Lally Tollendal, who after having served from the age of twelve to sixty-four in every quarter of the globe, from Barcelona to Dettingen, and from Fontenoy to Pondicherry, was beheaded on the 9th of May, 1766. The Marquis De Lally Tollendal, a distinguished lawyer and statesman of the Bourbonist party, and writer of the life of Strafford, and many other works, was a grandnephew to James Lally, the member for Tuam in '89.

Colonel Roger Mac Elligot who commanded Lord Clancarty's regiment (the 12th infantry) in the Brigade was member for Ardfert.

Limerick.—Sir John Fitzgerald was "*col. propr.*" of the regiment of Limerick (8th infantry) in the Brigade.

Oliver O'Gara, member for Tulske, was Lieutenant-Colonel of the guards under Colonel Dorrington.

Hugh Mac Mahon, Gordon O'Nial's Lieutenant-Colonel, was member for Monaghan.

The Right Hon. Nicholas Purcell, member for Tipperary, was a Privy Councellor early in James's reign. His family were Barons of Loughmoe, and of great consideration in those parts.

The first bill introduced into the Lords was on the 8th of May—that for the recognition of the king, and the same day committees of grievance were appointed.

## CHAPTER IV.

### THE SESSION.

It is needless for us to track the parliament through the debates of the session, which lasted till the 20th July. The few acts (thirty-five) passed in two months, received full and earnest discussion; committees and counsel were heard on many of them (the Acts for repealing the Settlement in particular), and this parliament refused even to adjourn during any holiday.

We trust our readers will deal like searchers for truth, not like polemics, with these documents and with the history of these times. But, above all, let them not approach the subject, unless it be in a spirit enlightened by philosophy and warmed by charity. Thus studied, this time, which has been the armoury of faction, may become the temple of reconciliation. The descendant of the Williamite ought to sympathise with the urgent patriotism and loyalty of the parliament, rather than dwell on its errors, or on the sufferings which civil war inflicted on his forefathers. The heir of the Jacobite may well be proud of such countrymen as the Inniskilliners and the 'Prentice Boys of Derry. Both must deplore that the falsehoods, corruption, and forgeries of English aristocrats, the imprudence of an English king, and the fickleness of the English people, placed the noble cavalry which slew Schomberg, and all but beat William's immense masses at the Boyne, in opposition to the stout men of Butler's-bridge and Cavan. What had not the defenders of Derry and Limerick, the heroes of Athlone, Inniskillen, and Aughrim done, had they cordially joined against the alien? Let the Roman Catholics, crushed by the Penal Code, let the Protestants, impoverished and insulted by England, till, musket in hand and with banners displayed, they forced their rights from her in '82—let both look narrowly at the causes of those intestine feuds, which have prostrated both in turn before the stranger, and see whether much may not be said for both sides, and whether half of what each calls crime in the other, is not his own distrust or his neighbour's ignorance. Knowledge, Charity, and Patriotism are the only powers which can loose this Prometheus-land. Let us seek them daily in our own hearts and conversation.

The Acts and other official documents of James's Parliament were ordered by William's Parliament to be burned, and became extremely scarce. In 1740 they were printed in Dublin by Ebenezer Rider, and from that collection we propose to reprint the most important of them, as the best and most solid answer to misrepresentation.

The parliament which passed those Acts was the first and the last which ever sat in Ireland since the

English invasion, possessed of national authority, and complete in all its parts. The king, by law and in fact—the king who, by his Scottish descent, his creed, and his misfortunes, was dear (mistakenly or not) to the majority of the then people of Ireland, presided in person over that parliament. The peerage consisted of the best blood, Milesian and Norman, of great wealth and of various creeds. The Commons represented the Irish septs, the Danish towns, and the Anglo-Irish counties and boroughs. No parliament of equal rank, from King to Commons, sat here since; none sat here before or since, so national in composition and conduct.

Standing between two dynasties,—endangering the one, and almost rescuing the other,—acting for a nation entirely unchained then for the first time in 500 years,—this parliament and its Acts *ought* to possess the very greatest interest for the historian and the patriot.

This was the speech with which his Majesty opened the Session :—

*My Lords and Gentlemen,*

THE Exemplary Loyalty which this Nation hath expressed to me, at a time when *others* of my *Subjects undutifully misbehaved themselves to me, or so basely deserted me:* And your seconding my Deputy, as you did, in His Firm and Resolute asserting my Right, in preserving this Kingdom for me, and putting it in a Posture of Defence ; made me resolve to come to you, and to venture my Life with you, in defence of your Liberties, and My Own Right. And to my great Satisfaction I have not only found you ready to serve me, but that your Courage has equalled your Zeal.

I have always been for Liberty of Conscience, and against invading any Man's Property; having still in my Mind that Saying in Holy Writ, *Do as you would be done to, for that is the Law and the Prophets.*

*It was this Liberty of Conscience I gave, which my Enemies both Abroad and at Home dreaded; especially when they saw that I was resolved to have it Established by Law in all my Dominions, and made them set themselves up against me,* though for different Reasons. Seeing that if I had once settled it, *My people (in the Opinion of the One)* would have been too happy; and I *(in the Opinion of the Other)* too great.

*This Argument was made use of,* to persuade their own People to joyn with them, and to many of my Subjects to use me as they have done. But nothing shall ever persuade me to change my Mind as to that; and wheresoever I am the Master, I design (God willing) to Establish it by Law; and have no other Test or Distinction but that of Loyalty.

I expect your Concurrence in so Christian a Work, and in making Laws against Prophaneness and all Sorts of Debauchery.

I shall also most readily consent to the making such Good and Wholesome Laws as may be for the general Good of the Nation, the Improvement of Trade and the relieving of such as have been injured by the late *Acts* of *Settlement*, as far forth as may be consistent with Reason, Justice, and the Publick Good of my People.

And as I shall do my Part to make you Happy and Rich, I make no Doubt of your Assistance; by enabling me to oppose the unjust Designs of my Enemies, and to make this Nation flourish.

And to encourage you the more to it, you know with what Ardour and Generosity and Kindness the Most Christian King gave a secure retreat to the Queen, my Son, and Myself, when We were forced out of *England*, and came to seek for Protection and Safety in his Dominions; how he embraced my Interest, and gave me such Supplies of all Sorts as enabled me to come to you; which, without his obliging Assistance, I could not have done: *This he did* at a Time when he had so many and so considerable Enemies to deal with: *and you see still continues to do.*

I shall conclude as I have begun, and assure you I am as sensible as you can desire of the signal Loyalty you have expressed to me; and shall make it my chief study (as it always has been) to make you and all my Subjects happy."

These were the Acts of that memorable parliament.*

---

\* Where the Acts are given in full, they are taken from the edition of 1740, by Rider, the title of which is copied above; where the titles only are found, they are taken from
" *An Appendix to the late King James's Acts; containing an*

CHAPTER I.

An Act of Recognition.

CHAPTER II.

An Act for Annulling and making void all Patents of Officers for Life, or during good Behaviour.

CHAPTER III.

*An Act declaring, That the Parliament of* England *cannot bind* Ireland [and] *against Writs of* Error *and* Appeals, *to be brought for Removing* Judgments, Decrees, *and* Sentences *given in* Ireland, *into* England.

[§ 1.] WHEREAS His Majesty's Realm of *Ireland* is and hath been always a distinct Kingdom from that of His Majesty's Realm of *England*, always governed by His Majesty and His Predecessors, according to the ancient Customs, Laws, and Statutes thereof : And as the People of this Kingdom did never send Members to any Parliament ever held in *England*, but had their Laws continually made and established by their own Parliaments : So no Acts passed in any Parliament held in *England* were ever binding here, excepting such of them as by Acts of Parliament passed in this Kingdom were made into Laws here ; yet of late Times (especially in Times of Distractions) some have pretended, That Acts of Parliament passed in *England*, mentioning *Ireland*, were binding in *Ireland;* and as these late Opinions are against Justice and Natural Equity, and so they

---

*exact list of the Lords Spiritual and Temporal and Commons who sate in the Parliament held in Dublin, in* 1689. *To which is added, A Catalogue of the Titles of all the Acts passed in the said Session, and the preamble to the Act for restoring the old Proprietors to their Estates, &c., as it passed the House of Commons." Dublin, Printed and sold by Ebenezer Rider, George's-lane.* 1740.

tend to the great Oppression of the People here, and to the Overthrow of the Fundamental Constitutions of this Realm. *And* to the End, that by these modern and late Opinions no Person may be further deluded, *Be it therefore Enacted* by the King's most Excellent Majesty, by the Advice and Consent of the Lords Spiritual and Temporal, and the Commons in this present Parliament assembled, and by the Authority of the same; *And it is hereby Declared,* That no Act of Parliament passed, or to be passed in the Parliament of *England*, though *Ireland* should be therein mentioned, can be, or shall be any way binding in *Ireland ;* Excepting such Acts passed, or to be passsd in *England*, as are or shall be made into Law by the Parliament of *Ireland*.

[§ 2.] *And whereas*, several Writs of Error were formerly Sued out and Retornable into the *King's Bench* in *England*, in order to reverse Judgments given in His Majesty's Court of *King's Bench in Ireland: And whereas* most of the said Writs of Error have been brought for Delay, and thereby many of His Majesty's Subjects of this Realm were greatly hindred from Recovering their just Rights, and put to vast Charges in attending such Suits in *England:* For the Prevention whereof, *Be it hereby Enacted* by the Authority aforesaid, That no Writ of Error shall be hereafter brought out of *England*, in order to remove any Record or Transcript of Record, out of His Majesty's Court of *King's Bench* in *Ireland*, or out of any other Court of Record here into *England*, in order to reverse any such Judgments.

[§ 3.] But in regard Judgments to be given in His Majesty's Court of *King's Bench* in *Ireland* may happen sometimes to be Erroneous, *Be it Enacted*, by the Authority aforesaid, That where any Judgment shall at any time hereafter be given in the said Court of *King's Bench* in *Ireland*, in any Suit or Action of Debt, Detinure, Covenant, Account, Action upon the Case, *Ejectione firmæ*, or Trespass first commenced, or to be first commenced there, other than where the King's Majesty shall be Party, Plaintiff or Defendant, or other Person or Persons against whom any such Judgment shall be given, may at his Election sue forth out of the High Court of *Chancery* in *Ireland*, a special Writ of Error to be devised in the said Court of *Chancery*, directed to the said Chief Justice of the said Court of *King's Bench* in *Ireland* for the time being, Commanding him to cause the said Record, and all things concerning the said Judgments to be brought before the Justices of the *Common Pleas*, and Barons of the *Exchequer* here, into the *Exchequer Chamber* in *Ireland*, there to be Examined by the said Justices of *Common Pleas*, and Barons of the *Exchequer*. Which said Justices of the Common Pleas, and Barons of Exchequer or any four or more of them by vertue of this present Act, shall thereupon have full Power and Authority to Examine all such Errors as shall be assigned or found in or upon any such Judgment as the Law shall require; other than for Errors to be assigned or found, for or concerning the Jurisdiction of the said Court of *King's Bench* in *Ireland*, or for any want of Form in any Writ, Retorn, Plaint, Bill, Declaration or other Pleadings, Process, Verdict or Proceeding whatsoever and other than for such Mistakes, Errors, or Failings, as are now supplied or helped by some Statute or Statutes in Force within this Realm. *And*, that any one or more of the said Justices and Barons, in the Absence of the rest, shall have Power to Adjourn the said Court, and continue the Proceedings of the said Writ of Error from time to time; and that after the said Judgment shall be affirmed or reversed, the said Record and all things concerning the same, shall be removed and brought back into the said Court of *King's Bench*, that such further Proceeding may be thereupon, as well for Execution as otherwise, as shall appertain.

[§ 4.] *And be it further Enacted* by the Authority aforesaid, That such Reversal or Affirmation of any such former Judgment shall not be so final, but that the Party who findeth himself grieved therewith, shall and may Sue in the High Court of Parliament in *Ireland*, for the further and due Examination of the said Judgment; anything herein contained to the contrary notwithstanding.

[§ 5.] *And be it further Enacted* by the Authority aforesaid,

That from the End of this present Session of Parliament, no Execution shall be stayed in the said Court of *King's Bench*, by Writ of Error or Supersedeas thereupon, after Verdict and Judgment thereupon in any Action personal whatsoever, unless a Recognizance with Condition, according to the Statute made in the 10th Year of the Reign of our late Sovereign Lord King *Charles* the First, shall be first acknowledged in the said Court of *King's Bench*. And *further*, That in Writs of Error, to be brought upon any Judgment after Verdict, in any Action of *Ejectione firmæ*, no Execution shall be thereupon or thereby stayed, unless the Plaintiff or Plaintiffs in such Writs of Error shall be bound unto the Defendant in such Action of *Ejectione firmæ*, in such reasonable Sum as the said Court of *King's Bench* shall think fit, with Condition, that if the Judgment shall be affirmed in the said Writ of Error, or be discontinued in Default of the Plaintiff or Plaintiffs therein, or that the Plaintiff or Plaintiffs be Nonsuited in such Writs of Error, that then the said Plaintiff or Plaintiffs shall pay such Costs, Damages, Sum and Sums of Money as shall be awarded upon or after such Judgment affirmed, or Discontinuance or Nonsuit had.

[§ 6.] And to the end, that the same Sum and Sums and Damages may be asertained, *Be it further Enacted* by the Authority aforesaid, That the said Court of *King's Bench*, upon such Affirmation, Discontinuance, or Nonsuit, shall issue a Writ to enquire as well of the Mesne Profits, as of the Damages by any Waste committed after the first Judgment in *Ejectione firmæ*, and upon the Retorn thereof Judgment shall be given and Execution awarded for such Mesne Profits and Damages, and also for the Cost of Suit.

[§ 7.] *And whereas* of late Times several Persons have brought Appeals before the House of Lords in *England*, in order to reverse Decrees granted in the High Court of *Chancery* in *Ireland*, which tend to the great Trouble, Charge and Vexation of such of His Majesty's Subjects as have obtained such Decrees, and is an apparent new Encroachment upon the Fundamental Constitutions of this Realm, and also Appeal before Delegates in *England; Be it further Enacted* by the Authority aforesaid, That no Person or Persons whatsoever, do hereafter presume to sue out any such Appeals, or to tender or produce any such Appeal to the Lord Chancellor, or Lord Keeper of *Ireland*, or to any of the officers of the said Court of *Chancery*, and that such Appeals shall be void; and that no Appeal whatsoever (to reverse any Decree or Sentence passed, or to be passed in *Ireland*) shall be brought into *England* either before the House of Lords there, or any Commissioner or Delegates of Appeal. *And*, that all such Appeals shall be disallowed.

[§ 8.] And for rendering this present Act the more effectual, *Be it hereby Enacted* by the Authority Aforesaid, That it shall be an high Misdemeanour in any Person or Persons whatsoever, that shall in drawing of Pleadings either in Law or Equity, or in any Bill of Exception to be Filed in any Court in *Ireland*, or that at any Tryal, before any Court within this Realm, shall deliberately insist, that any Act of Parliament made, or to be made in *England*, wherein *Ireland* is or shall be mentioned, is or can be binding in *Ireland*, though it should not be made into a Law here by any Act made, or to be made in a Parliament held, or to be held here. *And also*, it shall be an high Misdemeanour in any Person or Persons whatsoever, who within this Realm shall tender or produce any Writ or Writs of Error out of *England* in His Majesty's Court of *King's Bench* in *Ireland*, or to all or any of the Judges of the said Court for the time being, Retornable to the Court of *King's Bench* in *England*, or that shall tender or produce any Appeal to the Lord Chancellor or Lord Keeper of *Ireland* for the time being, or to any of the Officers of the said Court of *Chancery*, or to the Chancellor, Treasurer, and Barons of the *Exchequer*, from the House of Lords in *England*, or that shall tender any Appeal out of *England* to any Spiritual Judge or Spiritual Court, or Delegates within this Realm, in order to reverse any Sentence given in *Ireland*, by any Court of Delegates in *England*. *And*, that if any Person or Persons shall offend herein, he shall be Fined and Imprisoned, according to the

Discretion of the Court where he shall be Prosecuted for the same.

### CHAPTER IV.

An Act for Repealing the Acts of Settlement, and Explanation, Resolution of Doubts and all Grants, Patents and Certificates, pursuant to them or any of them. [This Act will be dealt with separately in the next chapter.]

### CHAPTER V.

An Act for punishing of persons who bring in counterfeit Coin of foreign Realms being current in this Realm, or counterfeit the same within this Realm, or wash, clip, file or lighten the same.

### CHAPTER VI.

An Act for taking off all Incapacities on the Natives of this Kingdom.

### CHAPTER VII.

An Act for taking away the Benefits of the Clergy in certain Cases of Felony in this Kingdom for two Years.

### CHAPTER VIII.

An Act to continue two Acts made to prevent Delays in Execution ; and to prevent Arrests of Judgments and Superseding Executions.

### CHAPTER IX.

*An Act for Repealing a* Statute, Entituled, *An Act for Provision of Ministers in Cities and Corporate Towns, and making the Church of St.* Andrews *in the Suburbs of* [the city of] Dublin *Presentative for ever.*

Preamble omitted.] *Be it therefore Enacted,* by the King's

most Excellent Majesty, by and with the Advice and Consent of the Lords Spiritual and Temporal, and Commons in this present Parliament Assembled, and by Authority of the same, that so much of the said Act, as extends to the granting, imposing, or securing the Duties or Payments of Twelve Pence in the Pound as aforesaid, be, and is hereby repealed; and that the residue of the said Act, relating to the making of the said Church of St. *Andrew's* Presentative for ever, and providing for the Building thereof, and for purchasing Lands and Livings for the use of the said Church, shall remain in full force.

## CHAPTER X.

An Act of Supply for his Majesty for the Support of his Army.

[The Act of Supply begins by giving good reasons for the making of it; namely, that the army cost far more than the king's revenue, and that that army was rendered necessary from the invasion of Ireland by the English rebels. It next grants the king £20,000 a month, to be raised by a land-tax, and this sum it distributes on the different counties and counties of towns, according to their abilities. The rebellious counties of Fermanagh and Derry are taxed just as lightly as if they were loyal. The names of the commissioners are, beyond a doubt, those of the first men in their respective counties. The rank of the country was as palpably on James's side, as was the populace.

The clauses regarding the tenants are remarkably clear and liberal; " For as much," it says, " as it would be hard that the tenants should bear *any* proportion of the said sum, considering that it is very difficult for

K

the tenant to pay his rent in these distracted times," it goes on to provide that the tax shall, in the first instance, be paid by the occupier, but that, where land is let at its value, he shall be ALLOWED THE WHOLE OF THE TAX OUT OF HIS RENT, notwithstanding any contract to the contrary; and that where the land was let at *half* its value *or less*, then, and then only, should the tenant pay a share (half) of the tax. Thus not only rack-rented farms, but all let at any rent, no matter how little, over half the value, were free of this tax. Where, in distracted or quiet times, since, has a parliament of landlords in England or Ireland acted with equal liberality?

The £20,000 a month hereby granted was altogether insufficient for the war; and James, urged by the military exigency, which did not tolerate the delay of calling a parliament when Schomberg threatened the capital, issued a commission on the 10th April, 1690, to raise £20,000 a month additional; yet so far was even this from meeting his wants, that we find by one of Tyrconnell's letters to the queen, (quoted in Thorpe's catalogue for 1836), that in the spring of 1689, James's expenses were £100,000 a month. Those who have censured this additional levy and the brass coinage, were jealous of what was done towards fighting the battle of Ireland, or forgot that levies by the crown and alterations of the coin had been practised by every government in Europe.]

## Chapter XI.

An Act for Repealing the Act for keeping and celebrating the 23rd of *October* as an Anniversary Thanksgiving in this Kingdom.

## Chapter XII.

An Act for Liberty of Conscience, and Repealing such Acts or Clauses in any Act of Parliament, which are inconsistent with the same.

*An Act concerning Tythes and other Ecclesiastical Duties.*

[Acts XIII. and XV. provide for the payment of tithes by Protestants to the Protestant Church and by Catholics to the Catholic Church; a settlement of the Church question fairer and more reasonable than the one adopted in our own day.—Editor.]

## Chapter XIV.

An Act regulating Tythes, and other Ecclesiastical Duties in the Province of *Ulster*.

## Chapter XVI.

An Act for Repealing the Act for real Union and Division of Parishes, and concerning Churches, Free-Schools and Exchanges.

## Chapter XVII.

An Act for Relief and Release of poor distressed Prisoners for Debts.

### Chapter XVIII.

*An Act for the Repealing an Act,* Entituled, *An Act for Confirmation of Letters Patents Granted to his Grace* James *Duke of Ormond.*

[The list of estates granted to Ormond, under the settlement at the restoration, occupies a page and a half of Cox's Magazine. To reduce him to his hereditary principalities (for they were no less) which he held in 1641, was no great grievance, and that was the object of this Act.]*

### Chapter XIX.

An Act for Encouragement of Strangers and others to inhabit and plant in the Kingdom of *Ireland.*

### Chapter XX.

An Act for Prevention of Frauds and Perjuries.

### Chapter XXI.

An Act Prohibiting the Importation of English, Scotch, or Welch Coals into this Kingdom.

[§ 1.] WHEREAS, It is Evident, that nothing could occasion the great Scarcity of Money now in this Kingdom, but the Extraordinary Industry that was used by Persons not well affected to the Government, to Transport considerable Sums of Money into *England, Holland,* and other remote Parts. *And whereas,*

---

*[The Act, however, makes no mention of estates or lands, but only of certain valuable "regalities franchises and jurisdictions" enjoyed by the Duke of Ormond in the County of Tipperary, now taken from him as a rebel.—T. W. R.]

it is likewise Manifest, that the great Quantity of *English*, *Scotch*, and *Welch* Coals, which were heretofore Imported into this Kingdom, hath not only hindered the Industry of several poor People, and Labourers of this Land, who might have Employed themselves and Horses, in supplying the City of *Dublin*, and other Places within this Kingdom, with Fewel, but hath likewise given Opportunity to the Persons Importing the said Coals, to see the said Places ruined for want of Fireing, when they pleased, or at least, to raise the Price of Coals so high, that the Poor should never be able to Buy; by means whereof, the said Colliers raised considerable Fortunes to themselves, and carried vast Sums of Money yearly out of this Kingdom, to the lessening his Majesty's Revenue, the ruin of several poor People, and the general Loss of the Inhabitants of this Kingdom; for Remedy whereof, *Be it enacted*, by the King's most Excellent Majesty, by, and with the advice of the Lords Spiritual and Temporal, and Commons in this present Parliament Assembled, and by the Authority of the same, That no Person or Persons whatsoever, shall from, and after the last Day of *August* next, Import, or cause to be Imported, any *English*, *Scotch*, or *Welch* Coals into this Kingdom, or any part thereof, for any cause, reason, or pretence whatsoever.

[§ 2.] *And be it likewise Enacted*, by the Authority aforesaid, That if any Person or Persons, shall, from, and after the said last Day of *August*, presume to Import, or bring any Coals into this Kingdom, contrary to the Intent and Tenour of the said Act, that then it shall, and may be lawful, to, and for the Commissioners and Governors of his Majesty's Revenue for the time being, to issue Warrants for the Person or Persons so offending, and him or them, to bring, or cause to be brought before them, or any Two of them, and if upon confession of the Party or Parties so offending, or by other undeniable Proof or Evidence, it shall appear to the said Commissioners or Governors, or any Two of them, that the said Person or Persons hath Imported any Coals out of *England*, *Scotland*, or *Wales*, into this Kingdom, that then upon such Proof and Evidence, the said Commissioners,

Governors of his Majesty's Revenue, are hereby Impowered, and Authorised to seize on the said Coals, and on the Ship or Ships that Imported the same, and the said Ship or Ships, with the said Coals, to sell and dispose of, for his Majesty's use, as to them shall seem convenient, any Act, Law, or Custom, to the contrary in any wise notwithstanding.

[§ 3.] And for as much as it may be hereafter thought convenient and necessary, to have Coals Imported into this Kingdom, and that we cannot at this time, fore-see the Necessity that may be for the same, *Be it therefore Enacted*, by the Authority aforesaid, That it shall, and may be lawful, to, and for the said Lieutenant, or other Chief Governor or Governors, and Council, whom his Majesty, shall, or may appoint for this Kingdom, at any time hereafter, at the Instance and Request of the Lord Mayor, and Common Council of *Dublin*, for the time being, to grant License or Leave to such Person or Persons, as he and they shall think fit and convenient, to Import, and bring into this Kingdom, such, and so much Coals, as the said Lord Lieutenant or other Chief Governor or Governors, and Council, shall, by their said License and Leave, to be Granted by them as aforesaid, think fit and convenient to allow, and no more, any thing in this or other Act contained to the contrary in any wise notwithstanding.

[§ 4.] And for as much as the Owners, or Proprietors of the Coal-pits of *Kilkenny*, and other Coal-mines in this Kingdom, may upon passing of this Act, enhance and raise the Price of Coals, to the defeating the Ends proposed hereby; *Be it therefore Enacted*, by the Authority aforesaid, that no Owner, or Proprietor of such Coal-pits, or Coal-mines, or Seller of Coals at any of the said Pits shall at any time hereafter, Receive or Demand more than *Nine Pence* for each Barrel of Coals (*Bristol* Measure) which shall be delivered by him or them, at any of the said Coal-pits, any Act, Law, Custom, or Ordinance, to the contrary, in any wise notwithstanding.

CHAPTER XXII.

An Act for ratifying and confirming Deeds and Settlements and last Wills and Testaments of Persons out of Possession.

CHAPTER XXIII.

An Act for the speedy Recovering of Servants' Wages.

CHAPTER XXIV.

[Printed in the Appendix to this Chapter.]

CHAPTER XXV.

An Act concerning Martial Law.

CHAPTER XXVI.

An Act for Punishment of Waste committed on Lands restorable to old Proprietors.

CHAPTER XXVII.

An Act to enable his Majesty to regulate the Duties of Foreign Commodities.

CHAPTER XXVIII.

An Act for the better settling Intestates' Estates.

CHAPTER XXIX.

An Act for the Advance and Improvement of Trade, and for Encouragement and increase of Shipping, and Navigation.

[§ 1] WHEREAS, this Kingdom of *Ireland*, for its good Situation, commodious Harbours, and great Quantity of Goods, the Growth, Product, and Manufactury thereof is, and standeth very fit and convenient for Trade and Commerce with most Nations, Kingdoms and Plantations; and several Laws, Statutes and Ordinance, having heretofore been made and enacted, and time to time, prohibiting and disabling the King's Subjects of this Realm, to export, or carry out of this Kingdom, unto any other the King's Islands, Plantations, or Colonies, in *Asia*, *Africa*, or *America*, several of the Goods, Wares, Merchandizes, and Commodities of this Nation; or to import into this Kingdom, the Goods or Merchandizes of the said Plantations, Colonies and Islands, without landing and discharging in *England*, *Wales*, or the Town of *Berwick* upon *Tweed*, under great Penalties and Forfeitures, not only to the Decay of the King's Revenue, but also to the very great prejudice and disadvantage of all the Inhabitants in this Kingdom, as well Subjects as Strangers; and which hath in a high measure contributed to impoverish this Kingdom, and discouraged several Merchants, Traders, and Artificers, to come from abroad, and dwell, and trade here: *And whereas*, the Increase of Shipping, and the Encouragement of Navigation, under the good Providence of *God*, and the careful Protection of his sacred Majesty, are the best and fittest Means and Foundations, whereon the Wealth, Safety and Strength of this Island and Kingdom, may be built and established. *Be it therefore Enacted*, by the King's most Excellent Majesty, with the Advice and Consent of the Lords Spiritual and Temporal, and Commons in this present Parliament Assembled; and by the Authority of the same, that it shall, and may be lawful, to and for his Majesty's Subjects of this Realm of *Ireland*, and to and for every other Person and Persons, of what Nation soever, residing and inhabiting here, during the time of such Residence, freely to trade into, and from all and every his Majesty's Plantations, Colonies and Islands, in *Asia*, *Africa*, and *America*, and to export from this Kingdom, and carry unto all and every the said Plantations, Colonies, and Islands, and there sell, dispose of, and barter all sorts of Goods, Wares, Merchandizes and Commodities, as well of the Growth, Product, or Manufactury of this Kingdom,

## THE SESSION. 57

as of any other part of *Europe*, commonly called *European* Goods, and import, and bring into this Kingdom of *Ireland*, all sorts of Goods, Wares, Merchandizes, and Commodities of the Growth, Product, or Manufactury of all or any the said Islands, Colonies and Plantations, without being obliged to land or unload in *England*, *Wales*, or the Town of *Berwick* upon *Tweed*, or entering all or any such Goods, Wares, or Merchandizes there; but as herein after is expressed, and without being obliged upon Shipping, or taking on Board, in the said Plantations, Colonies, or Islands, the said Commodities, to enter into any Bond, to bring the said Goods into *England*, *Wales*, or Town of *Berwick* upon *Tweed*, and to unload and put the same on shore, any Act, Statute, Ordinance, Law, Sentence, or Judgment, at any time heretofore made, given, or in force, to the contrary notwithstanding: *Provided* always, That the Master or Owner of all and every such Ship and Ships, Vessel or Vessels, so trading from this Kingdom, unto all or any the said Islands, Colonies, or Plantations, his or their Agents or Factors shall, and do before such Ship or Ships, Vessel or Vessels, sail from any part of this Kingdom towards the said Islands, Colonies or Plantations, perfect and enter into a bond, with one sufficient Security, to the use of the King, and to be perfected to the Collector, or chief Custom-house Officer, of such *Port* or Place, whence such Ship or Vessel is to sail, in such a reasonable Sum, as such Collector, or Custom-house Officer shall require, Regard being had to the Value of such Cargoe, as the said Ship or Vessel shall export, with condition to bring the Goods, Wares, and Merchandizes, which such Ship or Vessel shall take in, at all or any the said Plantations, Colonies, or Islands, into *England*, *Ireland*, *Wales*, or the Town of *Berwick* upon *Tweed*, and to no other Place, and there to abode and put the same on shoar, the danger of the Seas only Excepted.

[§ 2.] *Be it likewise Enacted*, by the Authority aforesaid, That all Goods and Merchandizes whatsoever, which shall be carried, conveyed, or exported out of this Kingdom of *Ireland*, to the said Islands, Colonies, and Plantations, shall be lyable and pay to the King's Majesty, his Heirs and Successors, in the said Islands, Plantations and Colonies, the same or so much Customs, Excise, or other Duties, as the like Goods or Merchandizes being exported out of *England*, into all, or any the said Plantations, Colonies, or Islands, and all Goods or Merchandizes imported into this Kingdom, out of all or any the said Islands, Colonies, and and Plantations, (Tobacco and Sugar only excepted) shall pay in this Kingdom to the use of the King's Majesty, his Heirs, and Successors, the same or like Duties, Custom and Excise, and no more or other, and in such manner, and at such time, and subject to such Penalties and Forfeitures, for Non-Entry, Undue Entry, or Non-Payment of Duties, as in the like Acts of Parliament made in this Kingdom, in the *Fourteenth* and *Fifteenth* Years of Reign of the late King CHARLES the Second; the One, Entituled, *An Act for Settling the Subsidy or Poundage, and Granting a Subsidy of Tunnage, and other Sums of Money unto His Royal Majesty, his Heirs and Successors;* the same to be paid upon Merchandize, imported and exported into or out of the Kingdom of *Ireland*, according to a Book of Rates hereunto annexed; and the other, Entituled, *An Act for the Settling of the Excise, or new Im-Post, upon His Majesty, His Heirs and Successors*, according to the Book of Rates, therein inserted, and as in the said Book of Rates, and as in the Rules, Orders, and Directions, to the said Acts and Books of Rates annexed, are contained and specified.

[§ 3.] *And whereas*, the Duties, and Custom, and Excise on Tobacco, of the King's Majesty's Plantations, imported into this Kingdom, amount to no more according to the said two late Acts of Parliament in this Kingdom, and Books of Rates to them annexed, but to Two Pence *per* Pound, which is too small a Duty; *Be it therefore Enacted*, by the Authority aforesaid, that all Tobacco of the Growth or Product of all or any His Majesty's New Plantations or Islands, or any Plantations belonging to His most *Christian* Majesty, imported into this Kingdom, out of all or any the said Plantations and Islands, shall from and after the Eighteenth Day of *July*, 1689, be charged, and lyable to pay unto his Majesty, his Heirs, and Successors, the Sum of Five Pence *Sterl.* for each Pound, Custom, and Excise, (that is to say Two Pence for each Pound Custom, and Three Pence for each Pound Excise, and no more ; *Provided* always, That *Spanish* and *Brazil* Tobacco, shall pay the same Duty of Custom, and Excise, as formerly ; and that likewise, Tobacco of that Growth or Product of the King's Plantations, or any of the Foreign Plantations belonging to his *Most Christian Majesty*, imported into this Kingdom out of *England*, or any other part of *Europe* at any time, from and after the Eighteenth Day of *July*, 1689, shall pay and satisfy unto the King's Majesty, his Heirs and Successors, the Sum of Two Pence, *Sterl.* Custom, for, and out of each and every Pound, and the Sum of Two Pence half-penny, *Sterl.* Excise, for, and out of each Pound and no more. *And*, That Sugars, Indicoe, Logwood, imported into this Kingdom out of *England*, shall pay, and satisfy unto the King's Majesty, his Heirs and Successors (*viz.*), white Sugar coming from *England*, Ten Shillings Custom, and Ten Shillings Excise for every hundred weight, and no more ; brown Sugar, the Sum of Two Shillings and Six Pence, *Sterl.* Custom, and the like Sum of Two Shillings and Six Pence *Sterl.* Excise for each hundred weight, and no more ; Indicoe, the Sum of Two Pence *per* Pound Excise, and Two Pence Custom for each Pound, and no more ; and Log-wood, Five Shillings *Sterl.* Excise, and Five Shillings *Sterl.* Custom, for each hundred weight, and no more ; The said Duties, Customs, and Excise to be paid in such manner, and under such Pains and Forfeitures, and with such Allowances as in the aforesaid Two Acts and Books of Rates, Orders and Directions are expressed and contained.

[§ 4.] And for the further Encouragement and Advance of the said Plantation Trade, and for Maintaining a greater and more firm Correspondence and Kindness between the Subjects of this Kingdom, and Planters, and Inhabitants of the said Plantations and Islands ; *Be it Enacted*, by the Authority aforesaid, That whatsoever Goods or Commodities of the Growth, Product, or Manufactury of the said Islands or Plantations, shall be at any time hereafter Unloaded, or Landed in any Part of this Kingdom, and shall pay or secure to be paid, the Customs, Duties, and Excise on the said Goods, due and payable, that at any time hereafter, within the space of One whole Year, to commence from the Day of such Landing, it shall, and may be lawful to and for the Merchant, Owner or Proprietor of such Goods and Commodities, his or their Agents or Factors, to export and carry out of this Kingdom into any other Nation, Dominion, or Country, such and so much of the said Goods and Commodities so landed, as he or they shall think fit; and that upon such Exportation the whole Excise of such Goods, which was before paid, or secured to be paid for the same, and one half of the Custom of the said Goods before paid or secured to be paid, shall be re-paid or allowed to such Merchant, Owner, Proprietor, his or their Factors or Agents so exporting, and that within twenty Days next and immediately ensuing the Date and Time of such Exportation, Tobacco only excepted.

[§ 5.] *And* for the more Encouragement of building good and serviceable ships, *Be it Enacted* by the Authority aforesaid, That any person or persons, who shall within the space of Ten Years, to commence the 24*th* of *June*, 1689, build or cause to be built within this Kingdom of *Ireland*, any Ship or Vessel above Twenty-five Tun, and under One Hundred Tun, Burthen, shall and may for the first three Voyages any such Ship or Vessel shall make out of this Kingdom, upon the said Ship or Vessel's Return from such Voyage back into this Kingdom, have, receive, or be allowed to his and their own proper Use one Eighth Part of the Duties of Customs and Excise, which shall be due or payable to the King, his Heirs, or Successors, for and out of all the Goods and Commodities so imported in such Ship or Vessel upon the said three first Returns, which such Ship or Vessel shall make into this Kingdom. *And* likewise, That any Person or Persons who shall within the said space of Ten Years commencing, as aforesaid, build or cause to be built in this Kingdom any Ship or Vessel exceeding in Burthen One Hundred Tun, shall for the first four Voyages such Ship or Vessel shall make

## THE SESSION.

out of this Kingdom, and upon the said Ship or Vessel's Return from the said Voyages back to this Kingdom, have and receive to his and their own proper Use one Eighth Part of the Duties of Custom and Excise, which shall be due or payable to the King, his Heirs or Successors, for or out of the Goods and Commodities so imported into such Ship or Vessel upon the four first Returns such Ship or Vessel shall make out of this Kingdom.

[§ 6.] And to the end that Masters of Ships, Seamen, Mariners, Ship-wrights, Carpenters, Rope-makers and Block-makers may be encouraged and invited to come and dwell in this Kingdom, and that thereby Navigation may improve and increase, *Be it further Enacted* by the Authority aforesaid, That all and every Masters of Ships, and Ship-wrights, Ship-Carpenters, Sea-men, Mariners, Rope-makers and Block-makers, who are at present residing within this Kingdom, or who shall or do at any time from henceforth come and reside in this Kingdom of *Ireland*, and shall pursue and follow his Trade or Calling, shall and may for the time and space of Ten Years after his or their so coming into this Kingdom, be freed, exempted and discharged of, and from all sorts of Taxes, and Cesses, Watch, Ward, and Quarterings of Soldiers and Officers in and throughout this Kingdom : *And* shall likewise have and be allowed his and their Freedom *gratis* in any Town, City, Seaport, Corporation or Borough, where he or they shall please to reside, and pursue his or their Calling and Trade.

[§ 7.] *And be it further Enacted* by the Authority aforesaid, That in the respective Cities and Towns of *Dublin, Belfast, Waterford, Corke, Limerick and Gallway* there shall be established, erected and settled, before the *First* Day of *December*, 1689, in each of the said Towns and Cities, and so continued for ever hereafter, a Free School for Teaching and Instructing the Mathematicks, and the Art of Navigation; in every of such Schools there shall be placed and continued one or more able and sufficient Master or Masters for Teaching and Instructing the said Arts : And that every of the said Towns and Cities, shall out of the Publick Revenue and Stock to them belonging, or otherwise, settle and secure a reasonable Pension and Stipend for such Master or Masters, to be paid them Quarterly during his or their Continuance in such Employment or Employments.

[§ 8.] *Provided always, and be it further Enacted* by the Authority aforesaid, that the said Duties of Custom and Excise of Tobacco of the Growth of Product of his Majesty's Plantations, shall be and continue payable to his Majesty, his Heirs and Successors, during the time, and so long as the new Duties in *England* of Custom and Excise on Tobacco, amounting to Five Pence *per* Pound, shall and do continue, and so long as this Kingdom of *Ireland* shall have a free and open Trade to and from the King's said Foreign Plantations, and no longer ; and whensoever the said Duties of Five Pence *per* Pound Custom and Excise shall cease and determine in *England*, that then the duties of Custom and Excise, payable for Tobacco imported in this Kingdom before the making of this Act shall remain, and be payable for ever thereafter to his Majesty, his Heirs and Successors, and no more or other, and this present Duty to cease and determine. *Provided* likewise, that it shall and may be lawful to and for all and every Person or Persons so Importing Tobacco from time to time, and at all times hereafter, to export and carry out of this Kingdom into any other Nation or Kingdom all or any part of the said Tobacco Imported, and that upon such Exportation out of this Kingdom, the whole Duty of Excise of the said Tobacco, and three half Pence *per* Pound of the Custom shall be allowed and re-paid the Merchant, Owner or Proprietor, his or their Agents or Factors so Exporting the said Tobacco ; so that there shall be and remain to his Majesty, his Heirs and Successors, but one Half Penny *per* Pound Custom for the said Tobacco so Exported.

## Chapter XXX.

An Act for the Attainder of Divers Rebels, and for the Preserving the Interest of Loyal Subjects.—(Dealt with our sixth chapter.)

## Chapter XXXI.

An Act for granting and confirming unto the Duke of *Tyrconnel*, Lands and Tenements to the Value of £15,000 *per Annum*.

## Chapter XXXII.

An Act for securing the Water-Course for the Castle and City of *Dublin*.

## Chapter XXXIII.

An Act for relieving Dame *Anna Yolanda Sarracourt* alias *Duval*, and her Daughter.

## Chapter XXXIV.

An Act for securing Iron-works and Land thereunto belonging, on Sir *Henry Waddington*, Knight, at a certain Rate.

## Chapter XXXV.

An Act for Reversal of the Attainder of *William Ryan* of *Bally Ryan* in the County of *Tipperary*, Esq.; and for restoring him to his Blood, corrupted by the said Attainder.

# APPENDIX TO CHAPTER IV.
## Chapter XXIV.
*An Act for Forfeiting and Vesting in His Majesty the Goods of Absentees.*\*

[§ 1.] WHEREAS, upon the general Defection of your Majesty's Subjects in *England*, several of your Majesty's subjects have deserted this Kingdom, and repaired into your Majesty's Kingdom of *England*, and elsewhere, thereby endeavouring to weaken your Majesty's Interest here, and showing an apparent Diffidence of your Majesty's Protection, most part of which Persons have actually taken Arms, under the unnatural Usurper in *England*, and diverse others of your Majesty's Subjects became Rebels and Traytors within this your Realm: And for as much as the said Persons have left behind them several Goods and Chattles, Stock, Corn in Ground, Debts, and Arrears of Rent, and other Chattles, and Personal Estates, part whereof hath been seized in your Majesty's name, or otherwise, by several Persons, who have not yet answered or accompted for the same to your Majesty.

\* [This act was passed the 18th of July, 1689. The seizure *in the country* parts was ordered on 1st March. No seizure took place in Dublin till 9th August "There being free transportation for England in March, the Custom-house quay (now Wellington-quay) became like a fair, and most of the absentee goods were for England; scarce any thing valuable was then left unless by the carelessness of the persons employed by the absentees." King also says, that the directions, both in Dublin and the country, were, "to inventory and take security for the forthcoming of these goods, and not to strip the houses, &c."—*State of &c.*, p. 413.

Numerous officers were appointed to dispose of these goods; but up to September '89, when we lose sight of them, they had not been disposed of.]

*Be it therefore Enacted*, by the King's most Excellent Majesty, with the Advice and Consent of the Lords Spiritual and Temporal, and Commons, in this present Parliament Assembled, and by the Authority of the same, That all Goods and Chattels, Corn in Ground, Debts by Judgments, Statutes, Bonds, Bills, Books or otherwise ; and all Arrears of Rent, belonging to any Person or Persons, in Rebellion against your Majesty, out of this your Majesty's Kingdom ; or belonging to any Person or Persons, that by any Act of this present Parliament, shall be adjudged and declared a Forfeiting, Person or Persons absent, and all other Persons absent out of this Realm, and that aid, abett, or assist, the said Prince of *Orange ;* Minors under the age of Seventeen Years, and such Person or Persons who are entituled to such Goods or Chattels, or Debts as aforesaid, in Trust for others, who are not absent, or joined with the Rebels ; and such Person or Persons, as for some reasonable Cause to be allowed of, and approved under the Hands of the Commissioners of your Majesty's Revenue in this Kingdom, or the major Part of them, within three Months after the Royal Assent given to this Act, always excepted and foreprized, shall from the *Fifth* day of *November* last, be, and hereby are vested in, and settled in your Majesty, your Heirs and Successors ; and that any Person or Persons, who since the said *Fifth* day of *November* last, have seized or possessed themselves of any Goods or Chattles, belonging, or pretending to belong to any Person or Persons, upon Pretence of such Person or Persons being in Rebellion, or absent out of this your Majesty's Realm ; and any Person or Persons, who since the *First* Day of *May* last, have received any Arrears of Rent or Debt, due to any Person or Persons, who are, or have been in Rebellion, or now are absent out of your Majesty's Kingdom, be, and are hereby declared to be Debtors and Accomptants to your Majesty, your Heirs and Successors ; and such Person or Persons, shall by Process out of your Majesty's Court of *Exchequer*, to be issued within Two Years, and no longer, be made Chargeable and Lyable, as in other Debts and Accounts by the Course of the *Exchequer* is used or accustomed.

[§ 2.] *And be it further Enacted*, by the Authority aforesaid, That for the more speedy and effectual Remedy, for Recovery of the said Goods and Chattles personal, seized upon, it shall and may be lawful for the Commissioners for Management of his Majesty's Revenue, or any Three of them, upon Information given unto them in Writing upon Oath, which Oath they are hereby empowered to Administer, to issue Warrants under their Hands and Seals, for seizing such Persons and Goods, as they upon such Information shall see proper, and upon hearing of such Person or Persons, and the Defence by him made, if any such Person so called, do make such Defence, to examine such Witnesses upon Oath, and judge and determine the Matter, and by Process, or other Warrant from them, to commit such Persons, or seize the Goods of such Persons condemned, until by such Committal or Sale of their Goods, which is hereby authorized to be done, the Sum or Sums adjudged, shall be satisfied and paid, the Privilege of Peers as to their Persons, always saved and excepted, and that the said Commissioners shall have Power for executing this Act in manner aforesaid, for one Year, from the *First* Day of *July*, 1689, and no longer ; *Provided* always, that nothing herein contained, shall be prejudicial to any of your Majesty's Subjects now in this Kingdom, that have not joined with your Majesty's Rebels or enemies, to whom any Debts by Judgment or Decree in Chancery, or upon Civil Bill at the Assizes, or any Rents or Arrears of Rent, were due, on or before the *First* Day of *May*, 1689, out of the Lands or Houses wherein such Goods or Chattles personal were kept or abided, but the same Goods and Chattles, shall be, and are hereby made lyable and subject to such Judgments and Degrees, in case, the said Goods were by the Sheriff seized, or the same distrained for the Rent, before the same Goods or Chattles were seized into the King's Hands.

[§ 3.] *Provided also, and be it Enacted*, by the Authority aforesaid, That Corn in Ground, belonging to such Absentee or Absentees, shall be lyable to yield to the Owner or Owners of the Ground, on which the same shall stand, if a Stranger, such Proportion or Sum of Money for the standing thereof as by the

Custom of the Country is due; *Provided* yet likewise, That nothing herein contained, shall be prejudicial to any sale, *bona fide*, made of any of the Goods or Chattles, aforesaid, to any Person or Persons, by such Absentee, Owner, or the Servant or Servants employed by him, for the Sale of such Goods or Chattles, in Case he or they have, *bona fide*, paid the Money contracted for upon such Sale which is to be proved before the said Commissioners, by such Person or Persons, when thereunto called by the said Commissioners: *Provided* likewise, That nothing herein contained shall any way be prejudicial unto, or charge any Tenant or Tenants, or Receiver or Debtor, who hath *bona fide* paid or delivered over, or accompted for such Sum or Sums of Money, and *bona fide*, paid or discharged the same to such Absentees or such Persons, as the same was ordered for, or assigned unto, and prove the same before the said Commissioners, when thereunto summoned.

[§ 4.] *Provided always and be it enacted*, by the Authority aforesaid, That where such Absentees or Persons Attainted, did owe any Sum or Sums of Money, for Quit-rent or Crown-rent, that then and in such case such Quit-rent and Crown-rent shall be first paid out of such Goods and Chattles.*

---

* In March, April *and* May, *before the Parliament sate, Persons appointed by the Commissioners, came to all Absentees' Houses, and seized what Goods they pleased, and carried them away, unless Persons of good Credit appeared, and gave security to be forthcoming for them; and accordingly afterwards they were forced to deliver them to the Commissioners Orders, without any information or Oath made by any Person, as this Act prescribes; the Commissioners after it was passed, not only seized Goods of Persons who were no Absentees, on suspicion, and kept them until the Owners swore they were their own proper Goods; but they also without any Information or Oath made, sent for Absentees' Servants, and because they would not discover their Masters' Goods and Debts upon Oath, to Personal Interogatories of their own framing, committed them to Gaol.*—Note to Edition of 1740.

## CHAPTER V.

### REPEAL OF THE ACT OF SETTLEMENT.

It appears from the Journal of the proceedings of the parliament, and from many other authorities, that no act of the Irish Parliament of 1689, received such full consideration as the following. Two bills were brought in for the purpose of repealing the acts of settlement—that into the House of Lords, on May 13, by Chief Justice Nugent,—that into the House of Commons, by Lord Riverstown and Colonel Mac-Carthy. Committees sat to inquire into the effects of the bills, many memorials were read and considered, counsel were heard, both generally on the bills, and on their effects on individuals, the debates were long, and it was not till after several conferences between the two houses that the act passed. The act was deliberately and maturely considered.

The titles, and some of the effects of the acts of settlement, are given in the preamble to the following statute. The effect of those acts of settlement had been, in a great degree, to confirm the unprincipled distribution of Irish property, made by Cromwell's government, amongst those who had served it best, or, what meant nearly the same thing, who had most injured the Irish. The acts of settlement gave legality to a revolution which transferred the lands of the natives to military colonists. The repeal of those acts, within 24 years after they passed, and within about 37 years after that revolution took place, cannot excite much surprise. The *one-third* of their holdings (which the Cromwellian soldiers were obliged by the acts of the settlement to give up,) could not have made a fund to reprize those who had been ousted from the entire. However, the giving up of that one-third was not strictly enforced, and the stock resulting was wasted by commissioners, and distributed as the applicants had interest at court, not as they had title to the lands. Thus, lord Ormond got some HUNDRED THOUSAND acres; albeit he had done more substantial injury to the Irish, and to the royalist cause in which they foolishly embarked, than any of the parliamentarians, from Coote to Ireton. Under such circumstances, we are not exaggerating the effect of the acts of settlement, passed after the Restoration, in saying, that they confirmed by law the Cromwellian robbery. The testimony of all the credible writers of the time goes to the same effect. Indeed, the repeal of the acts of settlement would have been against the interests of the natives, if they had received justice from those acts. This, in itself, is sufficient to prove how much hardship they had caused. The repeal of those acts by the Irish, as soon as they were in power, seems natural, considering how great and how recent was the injury they inflicted. Still, as we said, 24 years had passed since those acts had become law. Many persons had got possession of properties under that law, and many of those properties had, doubtless, been sold, leased, subdivided, improved, and incumbered, upon the faith of that law. It might be urged that persons interested by such means in these properties, had become so with full knowledge that they had been acquired by violence and injustice, and that the original owners and their families were in existence, ready and resolved to take the first opportunity of regaining their rights. Such reasoning fixes all who had advanced money, made purchases, or become in any wise interested under the acts of settlement, with such injustice and imprudence as to diminish their claim for compensation upon the repeal of those acts. But it only diminished, it did not destroy that claim. All those persons reposed some confidence in the security of the then existing government; and many of them found a justification for the Cromwellian conquest, in the conduct of the Irish, as the well-sustained falsehoods of the English describe it.

For these reasons, Chief Justice Keating prepared a long memorial, which Forbes, lord Granard, presented to the king, during the discussions on the bills, in

May, 1689, setting forth the claims of those who came in under the acts of settlement, as incumbrancers, purchasers, tenants, by marriage, &c. This memorial is dishonestly represented by the Whig writers, as directed against the repeal altogether; but any one who reads it (which he can do in the appendix to Harris's life of William) will find that it is an argument in favour of the classes described in the last sentence. From the long and careful clauses in the following act, for the reprisal and compensation of those classes, we must infer that Keating's memorial produced its intended effect. However, these clauses require to be carefully examined, to see whether they carry out this principle of compensation fairly and impartially. The character of this parliament for moderation depends greatly on their doings in this respect.

We now come to a second class, the Irish who, having been given the alternative of "Hell or Connaught" (as a certain bishop was of Heaven or Dungarvan,) preferred the latter, and were located on the lands of the Connaught people. This class would generally come in for their old holdings in the other provinces, and required no compensation; but the distribution, under this act, of the incumbrances, &c., between them and the owners of their former and present lands, seems lawyer-like and reasonable.

The next great class are the "adventurers," those

who got lands during the Commonwealth, and whose holdings were confirmed by the settlement. Their claim was boldly and ably urged by Anthony Dopping, bishop of Meath. His speech on the Repeal Bill is given in King's appendix, and is worth reading. He bases their claim upon the supposition of the Irish having been bloody rebels, rightly punished by the giving of their lands to their loyal conquerors. His speech gives the genuine opinion of the English at the time. The preamble to the following act, and that to the Commons' bill, give the Irish view of the war. These documents deny that the bulk of the Irish were engaged in the conspiracy of 1641; and the denial is true, although it is also true that more than a "few indigent persons" engaged in it, as is plain from lord Maguire's narrative; and although it might have more become this Irish parliament to proclaim the absolute justice of the rising of 1641, on account of the sufferings of all ranks of Irish, in property, and in political and religious rights; while they might have lamented that English atrocities had led to a cruel retaliation, though one infinitely less than it has been represented. However, the parliament, probably from delicacy to the king, based the rights of the Irish upon the peace of 1648, and the Restoration as restoring them to their loyalty, and to the properties possessed in 1641.

Most fair inquirers will allow the justice of this restoration of the Irish; but will lament that the act before us contains no provision for the families of those adventurers, who, however guilty when they came into the country, had been in it for from thirty to forty years, and had time and some citizenship in their favour. There had been sound policy in that too, but it was not done; and though the open hostility of most of those adventurers to the government—though the wants and urgency of the old proprietors, added to a lively recollection of the horrors which thronged about their advent, may be urged in favour of leaving them to work out their own livelihood by hard industry, or to return to England, we cannot be quite reconciled to the wisdom of the course. Yet, let any one who finds himself eager to condemn the Irish Parliament on this account, read over the facts that led to it, namely; the conquest of Leinster before the Reformation; the settlements of Munster and Ulster, under Elizabeth and James; the governments of Strafford, and Parsons, and Borlace, Cromwell's and Ireton's conquest, the effects of the acts of settlement, and the false-plot reign of Charles II.; let them, we say, read these, and be at least moderate in censuring the Parliament of 1689.

*The Preamble to the Act of Repeal of the Acts of Settlement and Explanation, &c., as it passed the House of Commons.\**

\* This Preamble is James II.'s own writing, as appears by "The Journal."

WHEREAS the Ambition and Avarice of the Lords Justices ruling over this your Kingdom, in 1641, did engage them to gather a malignant Party and Cabal of the then Privy Council contrary to their sworn Faith and natural Allegiance, in a secret Intelligence and traiterous Combination, with the Puritan Sectaries in the Realm of *Great Britain*, against their lawful and undoubted Sovereign, his Peace, Crown and Dignity, the Malice of which made it soon manifest in the Nature and Tendency of their Proceedings; their untimely Prorogations of a loyal unanimous Parliament, and thereby making void, and disappointing the Effects of many seasonable Votes, Bills and Addresses which, passed into Laws, had certainly secured the Peace and Tranquility of this Kingdom, by binding to his Majesty the Hearts of his *Irish* Subjects, as well by the Tyes of Affection and Gratitude, as Duty and Allegiance there. The said Lords Justices traitorously disbanding his Majesty's well assured Catholick Forces, when his Person and Monarchy were exposed to the said Rebel Sectaries, then marching in hostile Arms to dispoil him of his Power, Dominion and Life; their immediate calling into the Place and Stead of those his Majesty's faithful disbanded Forces, a formidable Body of disciplined Troops allied and confederated in Cause, Nation and Principles with those Rebel Sectaries; their unwarrantable Entertainment of those Troops in this Kingdom, to the draining of his Majesty's Treasury, and Terror of his Catholick Subjects, then openly menaced by them the aforesaid Lords Justices with a Massacre and total Extirpation, their bloody Prosecution of that Menace, in the Slaughter of many innocent Persons, thereby affrighting and compelling others in despair of Protection, from their Government, to unite and take Arms for their necessary Defence, and Preservation of their Lives; their unpardonable Prevarication from his Majesty's Orders to them, in retrenching the Time by him graciously given to his Subjects so compelled into Arms of returning to their Duty; and stinting the General Pardon to such only as had no Freehold Estates to make Forfeitures of; their pernicious Arts in way-laying, exchanging and wickedly depriving all Intercourse by Letters, Expresses, and other Communication and Privity betwixt your said Royal Father and his much abused People; their insolent and barbarous Application of Racks and other Engines of Torture to Sir *John Read*, his then Majesty's sworn menial Servant, and that upon their own conscious Suspicions of his being intrusted with the too just Complaints of the persecuted Catholick aforesaid; their diabolical Malice and Craft, in essaying by Promises and Threats, to draw from him, the said *Read*, in his Torments, a false and impious Accusation of his Master and Sovereign as being the Author and Promoter of the then Commotion, so manifestly procured, and by themselves industriously spread.

And whereas a late eminent Minister of State, for

parallel Causes and Ends, pursuing the Steps of the aforesaid Lords Justices, hath by his Interest and Power, cherished and supported a Fanatical Republican Party, which heretofore opposed, put to flight, and chased out of this your Kingdom of *Ireland*, the Royal Authority lodged in his Person, and to transfer the calamitous Consequences of his fatal Conduct from himself, upon your trusty *Roman* Catholick Subjects, to the Breach of publick Faith solemnly given and proclaimed in the Name of our late Sovereign, interposed betwixt them and his late Majesty's general Indulgence and Pardon, and wrought their Exclusion from that Indemnity in their Estates, which by the said publick Faith is specially provided for, and since hath been extended to the most bloody and execrable Traitors, few only excepted by Name in all your Realms and Dominions. And further, to exclude from all Relief, and even Access of Admittance to Justice to your said *Irish* Catholick People, and to secure to himself and his Posterity, his vast Share of their Spoils; he the said eminent Minister did against your sacred Brother's Royal Promise and Sanction aforesaid, advise and pursuade his late Majesty to give, and accordingly obtained his Royal Assent to two several Acts. The one intituled, *An Act for the better Execution of his Majesty's gracious Declaration for the Settlement of this Kingdom of* Ireland, *and Satisfaction of the several Interests of Adventurers, Soldiers, and other his Majesty's Subjects there.* Which Act was so passed at a Parliament held in this Kingdom, in the 14th and 15th Years of his Reign. And the other, An Act intituled, *An Act of Explanation, &c.*

Which Act was passed in a Session of the Parliament held in this Kingdom, in the 17th and 18th Years of his Reign, most of the Members thereof being such, as forcibly possessed themselves of the Estates of your Catholic Subjects in this Kingdom, and were convened together for the sole special Purpose of creating and granting to themselves and their Heirs, the Estates and Inheritances of this your Kingdom of *Ireland*, upon a scandalous, false Hypothesis, imputing the traitorous Design of some desperate, indigent Persons to seize your Majesty's Castle of *Dublin*, on the 23d of *October* 1641, to an universal Conspiracy of your Catholick Subjects, and applying the Estates and Persons thereby presumed to have forfeited, to the Use and Benefit of that Regicide Army, which brought that Kingdom from its due Subjection and Obedience to his Majesty, under the Peak and Tyranny of a bloody Usurper: An Act unnatural, or rather viperously destroying his late Majesty's gracious Declaration, from whence it had Birth, and its Clauses, Restorations and Uses, inverting the very fundamental Laws, as well of your Majesty's, as all other Christian Governments. An Act limiting and confining the Administration of Justice to a certain Term or Period of Time. and confirming the Patrimony of Innocents unheard, to the most exquisite Traytors, that now stand convict on Record; the Assigns and Trustees, even of the then deceased *Oliver Cromwell* himself, for whose Arrears, as General of the Regicide Army, special Provision is made at the Suit of his Pensioners. Now in regard the Acts above mentioned do in a florid and specious Preamble, contrary to the known Truth in Fact, comprehend all your Majesty's *Roman* Catholick Subjects of *Ireland*, in the Guilt of those few indigent Persons aforesaid, and on that Supposition alone, by the Clause immediately subsequent to that Preamble, vest all their Estates in his late Majesty, as a Royal Trustee, to the principal Use of those who deposed and murthered your Royal Father, and their lawful Sovereign. And furthermore, to the Ends that the Articles and Conditions granted in the Year 1648, by Authority from your Majesty's Royal Brother, then lodged in the Marquess of *Ormond*, may be duly fulfilled and made good to your Majesty's present *Irish* Catholick Subjects, in all their Parts and Intentions, and that the several Properties and Estates in this Kingdom may be settled in their antient Foundations, as they were on the 21st of *October*, 1641. And that all Persons may acquiesce and rejoyce under an impartial Distribution of Justice, and sit peaceably down under his own Vine or Patrimony, to the abolishing all Distinction of Parties, Countries and Religions, and settling a perpetual Union and Concord of Duty, Affection, and Loyalty to your Majesty's Person and Government in the Hearts of your Subjects, Be it enacted, &c.

## Chapter IV.

*An Act for Repealing the Acts of Settlement and Explanation, Resolution of Doubts, and all Grants, Patents and Certificates pursuant to them, or any of them.*

[§ 1.] WHEREAS, the Roman Catholick Subjects of this Kingdom have for several Years, to the apparent hazard of their Lives and Estates under the Royal Authority, defended this Kingdom, until at last they were overpowered by the Usurper, *Oliver Cromwell;* in which Quarrel many of them lost their Lives, and divers of them (rather than take any Conditions from the said Usurper) did transport themselves into Foreign Parts where they faithfully served under his late Majesty, and his present Majesty, until his late Majesty was restored to the Crown. *And* whereas the said Usurper hath seized and sequestered all the Lands, Tenements, and Hereditaments of the said Roman Catholicks within this Kingdom, upon the account of their Religion and Loyalty, and disposed of the same among his Officers and Soldiers, and others his Adherents; and though his Majesty's said Roman Catholick Subjects, not only upon the account of the Peace made by his late Majesty in the Year 1648, but also for their eminent Loyalty and firm Adherence to the Royal Cause, might have justly expected to partake of his late Majesty's Favour and Bounty upon his happy Restoration, which was then extended even to many notorious Rebels in other his Countries and Dominions, which would make amends for the Oppressions and Injustice they lay under for many Years in the Time of the said Usurper; yet such were the Contrivances set on foot to destroy his Majesty and Catholick Subjects of this Realm, that two Acts of Parliament passed here, the one Entituled, "*An Act for the better Execution of his Majesty's Gracious Declaration for the Settlement of his Kingdom of* Ireland, *and Satisfaction of the several Interests of Adventurers, Soldiers, and other his Subjects there.*" The other Act Entituled, "*An Act for explaining of some Doubts arising upon an Act Entituled, An Act for the better Execution of his Majesty's Gracious Declaration for the Settlement of his Kingdom of* Ireland, *and Satisfaction of the several Interests of Adventurers, Soldiers, and other his Subjects there; and for making some Alterations of, and Additions unto the said Act for the more speedy and effectual Settlement of the Kingdom,*" by which many of the said Catholick Subjects were outsted of their ancient Inheritances, without being so much as heard, and the same were distributed among Cromwell's Soldiers, and others, who in Justice could not have the least Pretension to the same, contrary to the said Peace made in the Year 1648, and contrary to Justice and natural Equity. *And whereas* it is now high time to put an end to the unspeakable Sufferings of the said Roman Catholicks. Natives of this Realm, (who have eminently manifested their Loyalty to his Majesty against the Usurper the Prince of *Orange*) and to remove the unparallel'd Grievances brought upon them under colour of the said two Statutes, which cannot be otherwise redressed, than by repealing the said Acts, and restoring the former Proprietors to their ancient Right, the compassing whereof is much facilitated by his Majesty's Royal Condescention to apply towards the Satisfaction and Reprizals of honest Purchasers under the said Acts, a great part of the Lands and Tenements forfeited to him by the late Rebellion and Treason committed by Estated Persons within this Kingdom, who contrary to their Duty and Allegiance, joined with the Prince of *Orange*. Be it therefore enacted by your most excellent Majesty, with the Consent of the Lords Spiritual and Temporal, and the Commons in this present Parliament Assembled, and by the Authority aforesaid; *And* it is accordingly enacted by Authority of the same, That the said two several Acts hereinbeforementioned, commonly called the Acts of Settlement and Explanation, and the Acts of State, or Act of Council, commonly called, the Resolution of Doubts by the Lord Lieutenant and Council upon the Acts of Settlement and Explanation thereof, and all and every Clause, Proviso, Article, and Sentence in them, and every of them contained, and all and every Grant, Patent, and Certificate pass'd by vertue of, or under colour or pretence of the said Acts and Resolutions, or any or either of them (except what is hereinafter preserved, or mentioned to be preserved), be and are hereby absolutely repealed, annulled and made void to all Intents, Constructions and Purposes whatsoever, as if the same had never been made or passed, notwithstanding any Mis-recital of the Title to them, or either of them, or of the exact time when the said Acts or either of them were made and passed.

[§ 2.] And be it further enacted, That all manner of Persons who were any way entituled to any Lands, Tenements or Hereditaments, or whose Ancestors were any way seized, possessed of, or entituled to any Lands, Tenements, Hereditaments, in Use, Possession, Reversion or Remainder in this Kingdom of *Ireland*, on the 22d Day of *October*, 1641, their Heirs or Assigns, and every Person lawfully claiming by, from, or under them and his and their Feoffees and Trustees, to and for their Use or Uses, or in Trust for them or any of them, and who were barred, excluded, hindered or prejudiced by the said Acts, Resolutions, Grants, Patents and Certificates, shall and may have and take such and the like Remedy by Action, or otherwise, for revesting or recovering the same, as they, or any, or either of them now might, could, or ought to have had or taken, in case the said Acts, Resolutions, or any Grant, Patent, or Certificate had never been made or pass'd, any Clause, Proviso, Article, Sentence, or Restriction in the said Acts, Resolutions, Grants, Patents or Certificates, and any Limitation of Time,

Descent cast, common Recovery, Judgment, or Non-claim upon any Fine or Fines, or upon any other matter or thing where an Entry or Claim could or would have aided him or them, or any of his or their Ancestors, Feoffees and Trustees, in any wise notwithstanding.

[§ 3.] *And* be it further Enacted by the Authority aforesaid, That all Attainders and Outlawries for Treason, or any other Offence; and also all Treasons and other Offences whatsoever upon account or pretence of the Rebellion mentioned or expressed to have begun or arisen in this Kingdom on the 23d Day of *October*, 1641, and also all Penalties, Pains, Forfeitures, Bars and Disabilities accrued, or supposed to be accrued thereby, or by any Means or Ways touching or relating thereto, or any way upon account or pretence thereof, be and are hereby made void, released and discharged to all Intents and Purposes whatsoever.

[§ 4.] *And* be it further Enacted by the Authority aforesaid, That every Officer and Officers, who have the Custody or Keeping of the said Attainders or Outlawries, or of any of them, or of any of the Proofs, Entries and Proceedings thereof, and of all or any of the Books of Crimination and Examinations relating thereunto, shall as soon as conveniently may be take the same off the Files, and from the respective Offices where the same do now remain, and cancel the same before or in the Presence of all or any of the Commissioners of Restitution herein mentioned; and any

Officer failing to do the same shall forfeit his Office, and also the Sum of £500 Sterling, the Moyety of the said £500 to be to your Majesty, and the other Moyety to any Person who shall sue for the same by Action of Debt, Bill, Plaint or Information in any of your Majesty's Courts of Common Law, in which Action no Essoyn, Protection, or Wager of Law shall be allowed.

[§ 5.] And to the end that every Person or Persons, and their Heirs, Executors, Administrators and Assigns who hitherto were barred, hindered or delayed from recovering or enjoying his or their just Rights, Titles, or Possessions by any of the matters aforesaid, may with all convenient speed be put into and be established in his and their Rights, Titles, and Possessions. *Be* it further Enacted by the Authority aforesaid, That such three or more Persons, as by your Majesty, your Heirs or Successors, by Commission under the great Seal of *Ireland*, shall be to that purpose appointed from time to time, shall be Commissioners to hear and determine the Claims and Title by *English* Bill of such Person or Persons, their Heirs, Executors, Administrators and Assigns, who are or ought to be restorable or entituled unto any Lands, Tenements, or Hereditaments, by reason of the repealing or making void of the said several Acts and Resolutions of Doubts, Grants, Letters Patents, Certificates, or any other matter or thing herein before mentioned to be made void, repealed, released, or discharged. And further, That the said Commissioners, or any three, or more of them, shall appoint certain Times and Places from time to time for their Sitting, Hearing and Determining the Rights, Titles and Claims aforesaid, and shall issue Summons to the Tenants and Possessors of the Lands claimed before them, and for Witnesses, and upon Appearance, or in Default of Appearance, then to proceed and examine the Right and Title of the said Claimant or Claimants upon Oath, which Oath they have hereby Power to administer, and to take Affidavit in Court or out of Court, and thereupon shall have Power to award Injunctions for putting into Possession such Person or Persons as shall appear unto them to be restorable unto, or who ought to be put into Possession of any Lands, Tenements or Hereditaments by vertue of this Act, and all Injunctions and Prohibitions to be granted to stop or delay the Proceedings of the said Commissioners shall be void and of none effect. But all Sheriffs and Coroners, to whom any Injunction or Injunctions for Possessions shall be directed, are hereby required and authorised at their Peril to execute the same. And the said Commissioners are hereby authorised to punish all Neglects and Contempts of Sheriffs, Officers, or any other Persons.

[§ 6.] And forasmuch as by reason of the several Oppressions, Distractions and Confusions herein before mentioned, and of the length of Time since the ancient Proprietors have been dispossessed, as aforesaid, the Deeds, Evidences, and Writings of the Persons restorable by this Act may be either lost or mislayed, so that the same may not speedily, or perhaps not at all be had, in order to make out his or their Titles before the Commissioners aforesaid. Be it therefore Enacted, that the Judgement, Decree, or Sentence of the said Commissioners, or of any of them, shall not be final or definitive; but the Person or Persons, and his and their Heirs, Executors, Administrators and Assigns, who is or shall be restorable by vertue of this Act, shall and may at his own Will and Pleasure, use and have his Action and Remedy in any of his Majesty's Courts of Law or Equity for recovery of his and their Rights, Titles, and Possessions, without resorting to the said Commissioners; or if he be not able to make out his Title before them.

[§ 7.] Provided always, and be it hereby enacted and declared by the Authority aforesaid, that this Act or any thing herein contained shall not extend, nor be deemed or construed to extend, to annul or make void any Release, Confirmation, Conveyance, Fine, Recovery or Agreement, made, done, suffered, perfected by any Person or Persons, or their Ancestor or Ancestors, who otherwise would have been restorable by vertue of this Act; but that such Release, Confirmation, Conveyance, Fine, Recovery or Agreement, shall be of such like force and effect as they would have been if this Act had never been made.

[§ 8.] *And* be it further enacted by the Authority

aforesaid, that where any Person or Persons who have been transplanted into the Province of *Connaught*, or County of *Clare*, or his or their Heirs or Assigns, has sold or conveyed away the Lands or Tenements there set out unto him in lieu of his ancient Estate ; and he or his Heirs shall notwithstanding such Sale of his transplanted Interest, be restored to his ancient Estate, or hath released his Right thereto, the said transplanted Interest be likewise restored to the Person or Persons who was or were intituled thereto the 22d Day of *October*, 1641, or to his or their Heirs or Assigns, that then the ancient Estate which shall be so enjoyed by or restored to the Person or Persons who sold the said transplanted Interest, or to his or their Heirs, or to any one claiming by or under him, or his Ancestors, or to whom he or they released the same. And likewise such other Estate as the said transplanted Person hath or had, or which came from him by Descent in Fee to his Heir or Heirs, shall be, and is hereby made lyable unto, and charged with the lawful yearly Interest of the Purchase Money, which was paid to the said Old Proprietor for the said transplanted Interest, by the Person or Persons who bought the same, the said yearly Interest, to be paid to your Majesty, your Heirs and Successors, after the Expiration of 21 Days next after the Feast of *Philip* and *Jacob* and *All Saints*, yearly, by even and equal Portions every Year, until the original Purchase-Money be paid unto your Majesty, your Heirs and Successors in one entire Payment; and the said Purchaser of the said transplanted Estate to be reprized in such manner as herein after to that Purpose is expressed, and the said Purchase-Money to be part of the Stock of Reprizals.

[§ 9.] And whereas by the Restitution of the Persons hereby intended to be restored to their said ancient Estates and Properties, which belonged to them, or their Ancestors, or those under whom they claim on the 22d Day of *October*, 1641, divers Persons who were Strangers to the several Persons to whom some of the said Lands, Tenements, and Hereditaments were distributed, came into the Possession of the said Lands, Tenements and Hereditaments by or under Purchases or Conveyances after the said Act of Settlement past, or before the first Day of *November* last, for good and valuable Consideration, and not consideration of Blood, Affinity, or Marriage, by or from the Person or Persons to whom the same have been granted or distributed, pursuant unto, or under colour of the said several Acts of Parliament, and Resolution of Doubts, or of some or one of them, and whereof Certificate or Patent hath been passed since the said first Act of Settlement: And likewise such Person and Persons, whose Ancestors, or themselves, or those under whom they claim, purchased the Estates set forth to transplanted Persons in the Province of *Connaught* and County of *Clare*, must be removed and displaced from their said Possessions and pretended Estates, and leave the same to the just Owners and Proprietors thereof, who are to be restored thereto by vertue of this Act; the said Persons so to be removed, are hereby intended to be reprized for such their Purchases in manner as hereinafterwards is expressed.

[§ 10.] And whereas an horrid and unnatural Rebellion was lately raised, and still is continued in this Kingdom, and in other your Majesty's Dominions, by great numbers of your Majesty's Subjects, and more especially by divers of the Persons and their Heirs, who had and enjoyed a great part of the Lands and Tenements which formerly belonged to your Majesty, and your Royal Father's and Brother's Catholick Subjects, and were given out or distributed by the late usurped Powers, as a Reward for their former Rebellion and Treason herein first mentioned, which said Rebels not being content therewith, but again endeavouring by the like Rebellion and Treason to draw in Foreign Forces, and to continue a Succession of Usurpation against your Majesty, and over your most Loyal Catholick Subjects of this Kingdom, in hopes thereby to gain the rest of the Lands, as they had obtained a great part of it before, and totally to deprive your Royal Majesty, and your Heirs and Successors thereof, and of the Crown and Dignity, divers of the said Rebels went into *England, Scotland, Wales, Holland,* and the *Isle of Man,* and other Places beyond the Seas, to invite and procure your most unnatural Enemy the *Prince of Orange,* and your Rebellious Subjects there, to send over Forces into this

Kingdom, while the rest of the said Rebels in great Multitudes arrayed themselves in Rebellious Number, and seized several of your Majesty's Forts, Garrisons and Magazines here for the *Prince of Orange,* and the said Confederate Rebels, whereby this your Majesty's Kingdom was in great danger to be lost ; but it pleased Almighty God, by the Courage and Conduct of his Grace, *Richard* Duke of *Tyrconnel,* your Majesty's Deputy in this Kingdom, with the dutiful Assistance of all your Majesty's Loyal Catholick Subjects here, unanimously joyning with the said Deputy to preserve the same for your Majesty, and to break and defeat the Measures and Machinations of a great part of the said Rebels and Traytors. And forasmuch as for the Treasons and Rebellions aforesaid, the said Rebels and Traytors have justly forfeited not only their Estates, Lands and Livings, but their Lives also. Be it therefore further enacted by your most excellent Majesty, by the Advice and Consent aforesaid, That all and every the Manors, Lands, Tenements, and Hereditaments, Use, Trust, Possession, Reversion and Remainder, Power of Redemption, and all and every Estate and Interest whatsoever in Law or Equity within this Kingdom, which on the first Day of *August,* 1688, or at any time since belonged or appertained to any Person or Persons whatsoever, who on the said first Day of *August,* 1688, or at any time since was in Rebellion or in Arms against your most Sacred Majesty either in this Kingdom, or in the Kingdom of

*England* or *Scotland*, or who corresponded or kept intelligence with, or went contrary to their Allegiance, to dwell or stay among the said Rebels, or any of them, or who was or were any way aiding, abetting or assisting to them or any of them, be and are hereby forfeited unto, and vested in your Majesty, and shall be deemed and adjudged to have been forfeited unto, and vested in your Majesty, as from the first Day of *August*, 1688, without any Office or Inquisition thereof found, or to be found, freed and absolutely discharged of, and from all Estates Tayl, and of all Remainders and Reversions, to the Intent and Purpose that the same may be settled, disposed, and granted, and confirmed in such manner as hereafter is expressed, (that is to say) that every Reprizable Person or Persons, his Heirs, Executors and Administrators, who shall be removed from any of the Lands, Tenements and Hereditaments, which are hereby to be restored to the ancient Proprietor thereof, as herein before is expressed, shall be reprized, and have other Lands, Tenements, and Hereditaments of equal Value, Worth and Purchase, set out and granted unto him out of the said forfeited Lands, hereby vested in your Majesty, for such Estate or Estates as the Lands from which he or they shall be so removed, were held by him at the passing of this Act.

[§ 11.] And for the most speedy and effectual granting of the said Reprizals, Be it further enacted, That if it shall be thought fit or necessary, there shall issue

Commissions under the Great Seal of this Kingdom, to such Commissioners as shall be named by the Lord Chancellor and Lord-keeper of the Great Seal of *Ireland*, within every of the Cities, Towns, and Counties of this Kingdom, to enquire and ascertain what Lands, Tenements, and Hereditaments any of the Rebels aforesaid were seized or possessed of, or entituled unto on the said first Day of *August*, 1688, or at any time since, and the true and real yearly Value thereof, and to make return thereof unto his Majesty's High Court of Chancery with all convenient speed.

[§ 12.] And be it further enacted by the Authority aforesaid, that such three or more Persons as your Majesty, your Heirs and Successors, by Commission under the Great Seal of *Ireland*, shall from time to time to this purpose appoint, shall be Commissioners for setting forth, allotting, and distributing the said Reprizals; which said Commissioners, or any three or more of them are hereby authorized and empowered to receive the Petitions and Claims of such Person or Persons who shall demand such Reprizals, in which said Petition and Claim is to be contained the Quantity, Quality, and the true yearly Value of the Lands, Tenements, and Hereditaments from which such Petitioner or Claimant was removed, and the Estate and Title he had therein, and the Quit-rents thereout payable, and the said Commissioners, or any three or more of them, to examine the Truth thereof

by Witnesses upon Oath, and such other Evidences
as shall be produced unto them; and upon due
Examination thereof, if they find that such Petitioner
or Claimant, or those under whom he claimed was a
Purchaser, by purchase made after passing the first
Act of Settlement, and for good and valuable Consideration, before the first of *November* last, and not
for or in consideration of Blood, Affinity or Marriage
from, by, or under the Person or Persons to whom
the Estate so claimed was granted or distributed, and
whereof Certificate or Patent was passed since the
said first Act as aforesaid, or that the said Petitioner
or Claimant, or those under whom he claims, was or
is a Purchaser for valuable Consideration of any transplanted Interest in the Province of *Connaught*, or
County of *Clare*, then to set forth unto such Petitioner or Claimant, other Lands, Tenements, Hereditaments of equal Value, Worth, or Purchase, and for
the like Estate as the said Petitioner or Claimant had
in the Lands, Tenements, or Hereditaments from
which he was, or shall be removed as aforesaid. And
the said Commissioners, or any three or more of them,
are hereby required and authorized to grant their
Certificates under their Hands and Seals to the said
Petitioner or Claimant, expressing the Denominations,
Quantity and Quality, and Number of Acres of the
said Lands so allotted, and the Barony and County
wherein the same do lie, and the Estate thereof to be
granted, and the Rent thereout to be reserved; upon

producing of which Certificate the Lord Chancellor or Lord-keeper of the Great Seal of *Ireland* is hereby authorised and empowered, without any further Warrant, to cause effectual Letters Patents to be made and passed to the said Claimant of the Lands so certified, to be allotted unto him, and under the Rents and for such Estate and Estates as in the said Certificate shall be to that purpose expressed.

[§ 13.] Provided always and be it further enacted by the Authority aforesaid, that such Person or Persons as shall claim or demand any Reprizals for any transplanted Estate or Interest, shall, before he or they have any Reprizal or Reprizals for the same allotted or set out to them, make full and true Discovery and Proof of the whole original Purchase-Money which was paid for the said transplanted Estate by the first Purchaser thereof to the Person or Persons, or his Heirs, to whom the said Estate was originally set forth or allotted by way of Transplantation ; and the said Commissioners, upon due Examination and Proof of the said Purchase-Money, are to certify the Quality thereof, and the Estate of the ancient Proprietor, which is to stand charged with the Yearly Interest thereof into your Majesty's Court of Exchequer, to the end that the same may be levied as it shall grow due from time to time, until the original Purchase-Money be paid in one entire Payment to your Majesty, your Heirs and Successors, the said Principal and Interest to be paid towards Reprizals, as aforesaid.

[§ 14.] And be it further Enacted, That in case at any time hereafter it shall be discovered, that any Person or Persons so claiming Reprisals for any such transplanted Interest, hath not discovered the full Purchase-Money first paid for the said transplanted Estate, but hath concealed any part thereof, then and in such Case the Person or Persons who hath so concealed any part of the said Purchase-Money, sha'l forfeit double the Sum concealed or not discovered, the one Moyety of such Forfeiture shall be to your Majesty, your Heirs, and Successors, and the other Moyety to such Person and Persons as shall sue for the same by Bill, Plaint or Information, wherein no Essoyn, Protection, or Wager of Law shall be allowed.

[§ 15.] Provided also, and be it further enacted, That neither this Act nor any thing therein contained, shall be deemed or construed to vest in your Majesty your Heirs or Successors, any the Lands, Tenements, Hereditaments or Chattles real, Right, Title, Service, Chiefry, Use, Trust, Condition, Fee-rent, Charge, Right of Redemption of Mortgage, Recognizance, Judgment, Extent, Right of Action, Right of Entry, Statute, or any other Estate of what nature or kind soever, which are hereby restorable, according to the true Intent and Meaning of this Act, to any ancient Proprietor, or his Heirs or Assigns, and the which have been vested or mentioned, or supposed to have been vested in your Majesty's said Royal Father and Brother, or either of them by vertue of both or either of the said Acts of Settlement, and Explanatory Acts, or Resolution of Doubts, or by vertue of any of the said Attainders or Outlawries, which are herein before repealed or made void, or mentioned to be repealed or made void; but that all and every Person and Persons, whose Titles, or whose Ancestors' Titles were hitherto thereby barred, forfeited, or any way prejudiced or interrupted, shall and may be restored thereunto, according to their Ancient Rights and Title, as herein before to that purpose is expressed or intended.

[§ 16.] Provided always and be it further enacted by the Authority aforesaid, that nothing in this present Act contained shall any way extend or be construed to extend to forfeit to, or vest in your Majesty, your Heirs or Successors, any Remainder or Remainders, Reversion or Reversions, for valuable Consideration, limited or settled by any Settlement or Conveyance made for such valuable consideration either of Marriage, or Marriage-Portion, or other valuable Consideration whatsoever upon any Estate, for Life or Lives, to any Person or Persons, who have not, nor shall not aid, abett or assist any Person or Persons in the Usurpation or Rebellion aforesaid, such Remainder or Remainders, Reversion or Reversions as are limited by any Conveyance, wherein there is no Power for revoking or altering all or any Use or Uses therein limited: And also such Remainder and Remainders, Reversion and Reversions as are limited upon any

Settlement, or conveyance of any Lands, Tenements and Hereditaments, commonly called *Plantation Lands*, and all Lands, Tenements and Hereditaments held or enjoyed under such Grants from the Crown, or Grant upon the Commission or Commissions of Grace for Remedy of defective Titles, either in the Reign of King *James* I. or King *Charles* I. in which several Grants respectively there are Provisos or Covenants for raising and keeping any number of Men and Arms for the King's Majesty against Rebels or Enemies, or for raising of Men for his Majesty's Service for Expedition of War always excepted and fore-prized; all which Remainders and Reversions, limited by such Conveyance, wherein there is a Power of Revocation for so much of the Lands, Uses and Estates therein limited, as the said Power doth or shall extend unto, and all such Remainders as are derived or limited of Plantation Lands, or other Lands held as aforesaid under such Grants made by the Crown, shall by Authority of this present Parliament be deemed, construed, and adjudged void, debarred and discharged to all Intents and Purposes whatsoever against his Majesty, his Heirs and Successors, and his or their Grantees or Assigns; and the said Lands, Tenements and Hereditaments belonging to such Rebels as aforesaid, shall be vested in his Majesty, his Heirs and Successors, freed and discharged of the said Remainder and Remainders, and every of them.

[§ 17.] And to the end the Reversions and Remainders saved and preserved by this Act may appear with all convenient Speed, Be it enacted by the Authority aforesaid, That the respective Persons entituled to such Remainders, do within sixty days next after the first sitting of the Commissioners for executing this Act, exhibit their Claims before the said Commissioners, and make out their Title to such Remainder or Remainders, so as to procure their Adjudication, and Certificate for the same, or the Adjudication and Certificate of some three or more of them. And further, That all Remainders, for which such Adjudication and Certificate shall not be procured at or before one hundred and twenty Days after the first sitting of the said Commissioners, shall be void, and be for ever barred and excluded, any thing in this Act or other matter to the contrary in in any wise notwithstanding; nor shall this Act extend to vest in your Majesty, or bar any Remainders limited to *Dudley Bagnel*, Esq. upon the particular Estate of *Nicholas Bagnel* of *Newry*, Esq. in *Newry*, the Lordship and Lands of *Mourne*, and all other Mannors and Lands now or lately belonging to the said *Nicholas Bagnel* in the Kingdom of *Ireland*; Provided the same be such a Remainder as was not, or is not in the Power of the said *Nicholas Bagnel* to bar.

[§ 18.] And forasmuch as we, your Majesty's most Loyal and Dutiful Subjects, always have been and for ever intend to be more studious and industrious to secure and advance your Majesty's Revenue, than to lessen or diminish the same : And whereas the Quit-Rents or King's Rents reserved, or now payable unto your Majesty, your Heirs and Successors, would determine by repealing the said Acts, if some Provision were not made to continue the same; Be it enacted by the Authority aforesaid, That all Lands and Tenements, which, by the said Acts of Settlement and Explanation, were charged with, or made liable to Quit-Rents, shall be, and hereby are charged with, and made liable to the same, or the like Quit-Rents, to be paid to your Majesty, your Heirs and Successors, as in and by the said Acts of Settlement and Explanation were appointed and directed, saving and reserving and excepting the Quit-Rents due and payable, and due out of the Earl of *Antrim's* Estate, which were granted to the late Earl of *St. Alban's*, and saving and excepting all such Lands and Tenements, whereof the Quit-Rents have been by Letters Patents under the Broad Seal of *England* or *Ireland* granted or released to the ancient Proprietor or Proprietors thereof, or to some Person or Persons in trust for them, or reduced into the Hand of the Ancient or New Proprietor, since the Acts of Settlement and Explanation, by reason of barren or unprofitable Ground, whether such Reducement was by Patent under the Broad Seal, or Certificate, or other Order of Commissioners, having Power to reduce the same; which Lands and Tenements are for the future to be charged only with such Quit-Rents or Crown-Rents as are by such Letters Patents, Certificates, and Orders respectively reserved and specified. And further, That all Lands which immediately before the passing of this present Act were not liable to any Quit-Rents, and shall be, by or pursuant to the present Act restored to the ancient Proprietor thereof; and likewise all Lands within this Kingdom, which being vested in your Majesty by this present Act, or by or upon account of the present Rebellion, or of any Treason committed by any Person since the first day of *August* last, shall be distributed or given out for Reprizals by the Commissioners for executing this Act, or otherwise granted by your Majesty, your Heirs and Successors, to any Person or Persons, Bodies Politique or Corporate, shall be and are hereby charged with and made liable to the same, or the like Quit-Rents to be paid to your Majesty, your Heirs and Successors, as in and by the said Acts of Settlement and Explanation were appointed or directed to be paid out of any other Lands in the respective Provinces where such Lands do respectively lie; so that the Rent formerly reserved to the Crown, on such Lands, exceed not the Rent hereby reserved; but where the Rents formerly reserved do exceed the Rent hereby to be reserved, the said former Rents only shall be paid.

[§ 19.] And be it further enacted by the Authority aforesaid, That all Arrears of the said Quit-Rents reserved by the said former Acts, which were due to your Majesty on the first Day of *May*, 1689, shall be answered and duly paid to your Majesty, and that your Majesty shall and may recover and levy the same in such manner, and by all such ways and means as you might have done, if this present Act had never been made, any thing in this Act contained to the contrary notwithstanding.

[§ 20.] And in regard the mesne Profits of the said ancient Estates, which are hereby restorable, are to be discharged, as hereafter expressed, Be it further enacted by the Authority aforesaid, that all Interests of Money for any Debt or Debts contracted before the 23d Day of *October*, 1641, and wherewith the Estate of any Person restorable by this Act may be chargeable, be and are hereby discharged and released for such Time as the Person or Persons, who should have paid the said Debts, were barred and kept out of their Estates by the said Acts or Rebellion; but the Original Debts are not to be discharged by this Act.

[§ 21.] And be it further enacted by the Authority aforesaid, That no Persons restorable by vertue of this Act shall sue for, or recover any mesne Profits of the Estate so restorable, but only for such mesne Profits as shall accrue or grow due after his demanding Possession, or commencing since for the Lands so restorable after the passing of this Act.

[§ 22.] And be it further enacted by the Authority aforesaid, that the Estate or Estates to be set out or allotted to any Person or Persons by way of Foreprizals by vertue of this Act, or any other Estate which he or his Heirs shall have, shall be lyable and Subject to all such Judgments, Statutes and Recognizances for Payment of Money, Rentcharges, Annuities, Mortgages, Dowers, and all other Estates, Uses, Trusts, Limitations, Settlements, Charges and Incumbrances of the Persons so reprized or removed, in such manner as the Estate from which he shall be so removed, would be lyable in case he never were removed from the same; but in case any Person hereby removable to make room for an old Proprietor, be a forfeiting Person, or is not intituled to have Reprisal, then in such Case it is hereby declared and enacted, that all and every Person and Persons, who, before the 7th Day of *May*, 1689, had any such Incumbrances as before is expressed, or any Judgment at any time before the 22d Day of *May*, 1689, on the said Estate hereby restorable to the old Proprietor, shall and may have Reprizals for the same out of the Common Stock of Reprizals, at the rate of Ten Years purchase: Provided always, that such Incumbrances, or the Reprizals to be had or allotted for the same, shall not exceed the Value of the Estate which was lyable thereunto, and which is restorable to the old Proprietor thereof, or to his Heirs or Assigns.

[§ 23.] And be it further hereby enacted, that where any old Proprietor, or his Heirs, who had or held any new Estate by Transplantation, or otherwise, by or under the said Acts hereby repealed, or any of them, shall by vertue of this present Act be removed from the same, that then, and in such Case, the ancient

Estate of which old Proprietor or his Heirs, shall be restored, And likewise all such other Estate which such ancient Proprietor, or his Heirs by Descent in Fee under him, shall have, be, and is hereby made Assets for the Ancestor's Debts, and lyable to make satisfaction for all such Judgments, Recognizances, and Statutes for payment of Money, and also for all Rent-charge, Annuities, Mortgages, and all other Estates, Uses, Trusts, Limitations and Settlements, Charges and Incumbrances of the said old Proprietor and his Heirs, in such manner as the said new Estate from which he or they shall be so removed would have been lyable, in case he or they were never removed from the same, except the Leases made by such Persons who are to be restored to the Lands they or any of them were seized or possessed of.

[§ 24.] And furthermore, for the prevention of the great inconveniences which may happen by the sudden removal of the Leasees, Farmers or Undertenants, from the Lands, Tenements, or Hereditaments whereof they are now in actual possession, and which are hereby to be restored to the ancient Proprietors thereof, their Heirs or Assigns. Be it further Enacted by the Authority aforesaid, that all such Leases in writing, of the Lands, Tenements, and Hereditaments hereby restorable, and which were made before the first Day of *May*, 1688, meerly in consideration of Rents, Duties, or other valuable Yearly Reservations, and not in consideration of any

Fine or Incumbrance, or of Blood or Affinity, and by vertue whereof the Lands, Tenements and Hereditaments thereby demised, are at this time enjoyed and held by the present Terr-tenants and Occupiers thereof, be, and are hereby made good and confirmed by the said Terr-tenants and Occupiers, for and during so much of the term or time in such Lease or Leases limited and expressed, as shall not exceed the Number of 21 Years, or three Lives yet to come and unexpired, and for all the Lands, Tenements and Hereditaments thereby demised, except that Messuage or Tenement which in the Year 1641 was the Mansion-house of the old Proprietor, or his Assigns; and except the demesne thereunto belonging (that is to say) the Town and Lands whereon the said Mansion-house then stood, and the said Tenant or Leasee, and his Executors, Administrators and Assigns for the Lands, Tenements and Hereditaments so by them to be held and detained by vertue of such Lease or Leases, are to pay the yearly Rent and Duties thereout reserved, or their just Proportion thereof, to the said ancient Proprietor hereby restorable, and to his Heirs and Assigns, and to give him or them Copies or Counterparts of the said Lease or Leases, and their own Obligations for Performance thereof, or otherwise to accept of a new Lease for the Lands, Tenements and Hereditaments so to be enjoyed, and under the like Rent proportionably, and for such time or time or term as shall be then unexpired of the said former Demise.

[§ 25.] And whereas in some Cases the Lease or Leases which such Leasee or Leasees had, might have been very beneficial Leases for a great Term, and originally made in consideration of Fines by them given to their Leasors for the same, or in respect of Improvements ; and as it is unequitable on the one side, that such Leasees should lose their Fines, Bargains and Improvements, without satisfaction for the same, so it is on the other side unreasonable, that the old Proprietor, who hath been hitherto kept out of his Estate, and is hereby barred from the mesne Profits thereof, should be obliged to bear the Loss and damage of Leases so made, at an under Rate and low Value : Be it therefore Enacted by the Authority aforesaid, that the said Leasor, his Heirs or Assigns, who is to be reprized for the said Lands, shall out of the Lands which shall be to him granted by way of Reprizal, make and perfect unto the said Leasee, his Executors, Administrators or Assigns, a Lease of Lands of the like Value ; and for such term or time of the said former Lease as will be unexpired at the removal of the said Leasor, and that the said new Lease shall be under the like Rents, Reservations, Covenants and Conditions, as in the said former Lease were expressed ; but in Case the said Leasor be a forfeiting Person, and not Reprizable by this Act, then the said Leasee and Leasees shall be reprized for their said Leases out of the Common Stock of Reprizals, according to the Methods herein before set forth ; but such Leases in Possession, and not now in any forfeiting Person, as were made by your Majesty of the Lands held by your Majesty under the Title of the said Acts, are to stand good and effectual at the Election of the Leasees, their Executors, Administrators or Assigns, and the Rent and Reservation thereof to devolve and come to the old Proprietors thereof, and particularly one Lease bearing date the first Day of *April*, 1675, made by your Majesty unto *John Keating*, Esq. ; for the Term of 26 Years, to commence from the first Day of *May* then next ensuing the date thereof, of the Town and Lands of *Blackrath*, in the County of *Kildare*, under the yearly Rent of £81 15s. Sterling, shall in like manner stand good and effectual, notwithstanding any Sale made by your Majesty unto him the said *John*, of the Inheritance of the said Lands or any Merger of the said Lease, but the Reversion and Rent of the said Lands so leased is hereby to come to the old Proprietor thereof, his Heirs or Assigns.

[§ 26.] Provided always, and be it Enacted by the Authority aforesaid, that all and every Person and Persons who is, or are at the time of passing this Act, seized or possessed of any Houses, Messuages, Manors, Lands, Tenements and Hereditaments, within this Kingdom of *Ireland*, and who are by vertue of this Act, or any Clause therein contained, to be removed from the Seizin or Possession thereof, or of any part thereof, shall have such reasonable and competent time given and allowed him or them for the removal of themselves, their Families and Stocks, as the Commissioners for Execution of this Act, or any three of them, shall think fit and appoint, not exceeding one Year from the first Day of *May*, 1689, and the same to be under such competent Rent, as the said Commissioners shall think fit to be paid to the Person or Persons, his and their Heirs, Executors and Administrators, who is, or are by this Act restorable to the said Houses, Messuages, Manors, Lands, Tenements and Hereditaments, any thing in this Act, or any other matter or thing to the contrary thereof in any wise notwithstanding.

[§ 27.] Provided also, and be it further enacted by the Authority aforesaid, that all and every Person and Persons who sow any Corn or Roots in any Lands, Tenements and Hereditaments, whereof they or any of them are now at the time of the passing of this Act seized or possessed, shall have, receive, and take the full benefit and advantage thereof, and have free liberty of ingress, egress and regress, for the making up and preserving, and of carrying away and disposing of the said Corn and Roots, or any part thereof as he or they shall think fit, he or they paying or allowing for the same to such Person or Persons as shall be restored to the said Lands so sowed with Corn and Roots, according to the Custom of the Country.

[§ 28.] And whereas there are divers poor and distressed Widows and Relicts, whose deceased Husbands, had they been alive, would have been restorable by this Act, and been thereby enabled to leave some Maintainance to their said Widows and Relicts; but in regard their said deceased Husbands, by means of the several Acts and other Matters herein before expressed and repealed, were kept from any Seizin or Possession of the Estates, which should of right be enjoyed by them, and for want of such Seizin, the said Widows and Relicts are not by the Common Law of this Land entituled to any Dower, and therefore are in danger of perishing: Be it therefore Enacted by the Authority aforesaid, That the want of such Seizin shall be no bar or prejudice to the Widows and Relicts aforesaid, but that every Widow and Relict, whose Husband, if living, would or might be restorable by this Act, shall and may have and recover such Dower or Proportion of her said Husband's Estate as she might recover by the Common Law, if her said Husband had a Seizin in Deed or in Law thereof, and the Commissioners for Restitution herein appointed, or to be appointed, are hereby required to cause the same to be set forth and allotted; or the said Widows and Relicts may, if they think fit, use and have their Remedy at Common Law; and if *Ne unque Seizie que Dower*, or any such Plea, shall be pleaded against any of them, it shall be sufficient for every such Widow and Relict to give in Evidence, that the Estate which her Husband should have had, was kept out of by any of the Acts or Matters herein repealed, was such whereof she might recover

Dower, in case he were actually seized, according to the Estate to him limited; and upon proving thereof, every such Widow and Relict shall recover, as well as if her said Husband had been actually seized of the said Estate; but such Widows and Relicts as had or enjoyed any Jointure to them limited, shall only have the benefit of such Jointures.

[§ 29.] Provided always and be it further enacted by the Authority aforesaid, That all and every the Honours, Manors, Lands, Tenements, Remainder and Remainders whereof *Robert* Lord *Baron* of *Kingstown*, now is, or at any time heretofore has been lawfully and rightfully seized or possessed of in his Demesne, as of Fee or Fee Tayl, to or of any Estate of Inheritance in Right of his Ancestors (that is to say) of *John* Lord *Baron* of *Kingstown*, or the Lady *Katharine* his Wife, situate, lying and being in the Counties of *Cork* and *Roscommon*, or elsewhere, within this Kingdom, and which hath been settled upon, or limited unto the said *John* Lord *Baron* of *Kingstown*, by his Father or Grandfather, Sir *John* and Sir *Robert King*, or by any of them, or to the said *John* Lord *Baron* of *Kingstown*, and the Lady *Katharine* his Wife, or to either of them, by Sir *William Fenton*, Knight, and Dame *Margaret* his Wife, or either of them, and whereof the said Sir *John* or Sir *Robert*, or the said Sir *William Fenton* were seized or possessed of respectively on the 22d Day of *October*, 1641, with all the Rights, Titles or Interests, which they or any of them respectively had thereunto, be and are hereby vested and settled in his Majesty and his Heirs, to be disposed of as his Majesty shall think fit, subject nevertheless to such legal and equitable Incumbrance, as the same would have been liable unto, in case this Act had never passed; any thing therein contained to the contrary notwithstanding.

[§ 30.] Provided always and be it further enacted by the Authority aforesaid, That the Capital Mèssuage, Town and Lands of *Chapellizard*, alias *Ized*, with all other the Appurtenances thereunto belonging and every part and parcel now at the passing of this Act, occupied, possessed and enjoyed as part or parcel thereof, and the Capital Messuage of the *Phenix*, and all the Houses, Messuages, Lands, Tenements and Hereditaments within the King's Park adjoining unto, or near this City of *Dublin*, in as large, free and ample manner as the same is now at the passing of this Act possessed and enjoyed by his Majesty, or any person claiming by, from or under his Majesty, shall be and are hereby vested in the King's Majesty, his Heirs and Successors, and shall be held and enjoyed by his Majesty, his Heirs and Successors; anything in this present Act, or any other matter or thing whatsoever to the contrary in any wise notwithstanding. And in case any Ancient Proprietor or Proprietors thereof hath, or have not been already satisfied for his or their Interests therein, that then such Ancient Proprietor or Proprietors shall be reprized according to his Title and Interest in the said Lands out of the forfeited Lands, according to the Rules of this Act.

[§ 31.] Provided always and be it enacted by the Authority aforesaid, That the Lord Chief Justice of his Majesty's Court of *King's Bench*, the Lord Chief Baron of his Majesty's Court of *Exchequer*, and the Master of the *Rolls*, or any other of his Majesty's Officers of this Kingdom for the time being, shall and may have and receive such Port-Corn of the several Rectories which have been formerly paid and received; any thing in this present Act, or any other matter or thing whatsoever to the contrary in any wise notwithstanding.

[§ 32.] And whereas in pursuance of an Agreement made and concluded between *Richard* late Earl of *Clanrickard*, and *Charles* Lord Viscount *Muskerry*, and *Margaret* Viscountess *Muskerry*, his Wife, Heir General of *Ulick*, late Lord Marquis of *Clanrickard*, several Provisions have been made and enacted in the said Acts of Settlement and Explanation for settling the Estate of the Family of *Clanrickard;* since which time several Deeds, Conveyances, Settlements, Provisions, Writings, Decree, Award and Agreements of, and concerning the Honour, Manor, Lands, Tenements, and Hereditaments, belonging to the said Family, or whereof *William* late Earl of *Clanrickard* was seized or possessed, were made and perfected by the said *William* late Earl of *Clanrickard*, or by his

Children after his Decease, or with their consent, which are not intended to be weakened or avoided by this Act; Be it therefore enacted by the Authority aforesaid, that the said several Deeds, Conveyances, Settlements, Provisions, Writings, Decrees, Awards, Agreements, according to the several and respective Estates, Uses, Trusts, Remainders, Limitations and Provisions therein mentioned, shall be and remain firm, valid in Law according to the said Award lately made between the Family of *Clanrickard* and the Limitations and Uses therein set forth; and that the several Deeds, Conveyances, Settlements, Provisions, Writings, Decree and Award to the Uses and Limitations in the said Award be of the same force and vertue, and in the same plight and condition to all Intents and Purposes, as if this present Act had never been made against the Heir General of *Ulick*, late Lord Marquis of *Clanrickard*, *Richard* late Earl of *Clanrickard*, and all Persons claiming by, from or under them, their Ancestors, or any or either of them, anything in these Presents to the contrary notwithstanding; saving the Right, Title and Interest of all Purchasers and Strangers, their Heirs, Executors, Administrators and Assigns.

[§ 33.] And whereas the Right Honourable *Hellen* Countess of *Clanrickard* having heretofore her Dower of the Estate of her deceased Husband *John Fitz-Gerald*, Esq. set out unto her, in which Dower several parcels of Lands were comprized, that did belong in

*October*, 1641, to old Proprietors restorable by this Act; It is hereby enacted, That the said Countess shall be reprized out of the other two Thirds of the said Estate late in the Seizin of *Edward Villiers*, Esq. and *Katharine* his Wife, in Lands of equal Value, Worth, and Purchase, that shall be forfeited to his Majesty for and during the Life of the said Countess to supply what shall be *bona fide* evicted from her by any such old Proprietors.

[§ 34.] And whereas by a particular Proviso in the Act, commonly entituled, *An Act for the better execution of his Majesty's Gracious Declaration for the Settlement of this Kingdom of* Ireland, *and, Satisfaction of the several Interests of Adventurers, Soldiers, and others his Subjects there* : It is amongst other things enacted That *Theobald* late Earl of *Carlingford* shall have, hold, possess, and enjoy to him and his Heirs, all those the Lands, Manors, Tenements and Hereditaments in the County of *Louth*, whereof the said *Theobald* late Earl of *Carlingford*, upon the First Day of *August*, in the Year, 1661, was possessed or set out, Assigned or Granted to the said *Theobald* by way of *Custodiam* or otherwise, in order to a further Settlement thereof to and on the said *Theobald* Earl of *Carlingford*, and his Heirs, for and in lieu of the Estate of *Coloony*, in the County of *Sligo ;* and also, That the said *Theobald* Earl of *Carlingford* shall have and enjoy, to him and his Heirs, the Manors, Lands, Tenements and Hereditaments, whereof *Christopher Taaffe* of *Braganstown*,

Q

and *Theoph. Taaffe* of *Cookstown*, or either of them, or any of their Ancestors, or any other Person or Persons to their Use, or in Trust for them or any of them, stood seized or possessed upon the 22d Day of *October*, 1641. And whereas the said Manors, Lands, Tenements and Hereditaments are by this present Act to be restored to the ancient Proprietors thereof, or unto their Heirs or Assigns; And also several other Lands granted unto the said *Theobald* Earl of *Carlingford* and his Heirs, lying and being in the County of *Meath*, *Sligo*, and *Tipperary*, whereby *Nicholas* now Earl of *Carlingford* will be a great Sufferer, if not otherwise provided for by this Act: Be it therefore enacted, and it is hereby further enacted by the Authority aforesaid, That the Commissioners for executing of this Act shall forthwith set out in Reprizals other Manors, Lands, Tenements and Hereditaments, forfeited unto, and vested in his Majesty by vertue of this Act, or upon account of any Attainder of Treason, of equal Value, Worth and Purchase with the Manors, Lands, Tenements and Hereditaments from which the said *Nicholas* Earl of *Carlingford* or his Heirs are to be removed or dispossessed of by vertue of this present Act, and which were held by the said *Nicholas* Earl of *Carlingford*, by vertue of the said Acts of Settlement and Explanation or either of them or by Patent or Patents upon the said Acts, and all and singular which Lands and Premises so set out in Reprizal, the said *Nicholas* Earl of *Carlingford* shall hold to him and his Heirs, at and under the same or like Tenure, Rents and Services, as all Purchasers are to hold by this Act the Reprizal set out to them or any of them, and subject to such Mortgages, Charges and Incumbrances, as the Lands from whence he or they are to be removed, were and are at the time of the passing of this Act; any thing in this present Act contained, or any other matter or thing to the contrary thereof, in any wise notwithstanding.

[§ 35.] Provided always and be it further enacted by the Authority aforesaid, That this Act or anything herein contained, shall not be Construed or Expounded in any Courts, either in Law or Equity, to vest in the King's most Excellent Majesty, his Heirs or Successors, or otherwise bar any Remainder or Remainders, or any Right, Title or Interest whatsoever, that ought to have descended or come, or which shall or may hereafter descend or come upon or to *Frances Lane*, now wife to *Ulick* Lord Viscount *Gallway*, by Vertue of any Deed, Will or other Writing whatsoever, made and executed by *George* Lord Viscount *Lanesborough* deceased; and that all the Right, Title and Interest whatsoever, in respect of the Premises, be saved to the said *Ulick* Lord Viscount *Gallway* and Dame *Frances* his Wife, this Act, or any thing therein contained to the contrary in any wise notwithstanding. Always excepted such Lands, Tenements and Hereditaments as were at any time withheld or detained from the Ancient Proprietor or

Proprietors on account of any Title derived or pretended to be derived from or under the said Acts of Settlement and Explanation, or either of them, and not under the Proprietors to his Heirs.

[§ 36.] And whereas by a particular Proviso in the Act commonly Intituled, *An Act for the better Execution of his Majesty's Gracious Declaration for the Settlement of his Kingdom of* Ireland, *and Satisfaction of the several Interests of Adventurers, Soldiers, and others his Subjects there*, It is amongst other things Enacted, That the Town of *Mullingar* in the County of *West-Meath*, with all the Houses, Castles, Lands, Tenements and Commons thereunto belonging and Forfeited to his late Majesty *Charles* the Second of Happy Memory, should be and were by the said Act settled upon the Earl of *Granard* and his Heirs, by the Name of Sir *Arthur Forbes*, Bart. according to a Grant thereof passed to him by Letters Patents under his said late Majesty's Great Seal of *Ireland*, bearing Date the 27th day of *July* in the 13th Year of his said late Majesty's Reign: And whereas the said Earl of *Granard* hath in Consideration of a considerable Marriage Portion, settled the said Town of *Mullingar*, with all and singular the Premises, on *Arthur* now Lord *Forbes* Eldest Son of the said Earl of *Granard:* And whereas the said Town of *Mullingar*, and all other the Premises, with their and every of their Appurtenances, are by this present Act to be restored to the Ancient Proprietors thereof, or unto their Heirs or Assigns, whereby the said *Arthur* Lord *Forbes* will be a great Sufferer, if not otherwise provided for by this Act. Be it therefore Enacted, and it is hereby further Enacted by the Authority aforesaid, That the Commissioners for Execution of this Act, shall forthwith set out in Reprizal other Manors, Lands, Tenements and Hereditaments forfeited unto and vested in his Majesty by vertue of this Act, or upon account of any Attainder of Treason, of equal Value, Worth and Purchase with the said Town of *Mullingar*, and other the said Lands, Tenements and Hereditaments from which the said *Arthur* Lord *Forbes*, or his Heirs, are to be removed or dispossessed by vertue of this present Act, or any Clause or Matter therein contained. All and singular which Lands and Premises, so set out in Reprizals, the said *Arthur* Lord *Forbes* shall hold to him and his Heirs, at and under the same, or like Tenures, Rents and Services, as all Purchasers are to hold by this Act, of the Reprizals, set out to them, or any of them, any thing in this present, or other Matter or Thing to the contrary thereof in any wise notwithstanding.

[§ 37.] And be it further enacted by the Authority aforesaid, That whereas *Francis Plowden*, Esq. is, and for several Years past has been seized in Fee of several Houses, Backsides, wast Plots, and Gardens, lying and being in the City of *Dublin*, and Town of *Gallway*, by and under the last Will and Testament of Dame *Katharine Plowden*, Relict of Sir *Daniel Treswel*,

Knight, deceased, he the said *Francis Plowden* having paid above two thousand Pounds Sterling in Debts and Legacies out of the said demised Premises pursuant to the said Will, that the said Commissioners for executing of this Act shall forthwith set out and allow in Reprisal unto the said *Francis Plowden*, his Heirs and Assigns, to his and their Use, Lands, Tenements and Hereditaments of equal Value, Worth, and Purchase with the said several Houses, wast Plots and Gardens for which the said *Francis Plowden*, his Heirs or Assigns, is or are to be removed, for restoring the ancient Proprietor by this Act any thing herein contained to the contrary notwithstanding: Provided always that *John Brown*, Esq.; his Heirs and Assigns, shall in Trust for his Creditors, and for support of his Iron-works, which are of publick Advantage to your Majesty and this Kingdom, have, hold and enjoy all and every the Furnaces, Store-houses, Mills, Dwelling-houses and Gardens, and other Improvements, built or made by him, or on his Account, in the County of *Mayo*, for his own, his Clerk's and Workmen's Dwelling-houses, and Conveniences to attend the said Works; and also all Dams built by the said *John Brown* for support of the said Works, with power for Repairs, as heretofore usually done, and next the said Works, and most contiguous unto them, so much of the Lands, which by the Rules of this Act would be taken away from the said *John Brown*, or his Heirs, and restored to the ancient Proprietors, as is or shall be necessary for the Gardens, Dwelling-houses, and Grazing for the Cattle and Horses of the several Clerks, Work-men and Labourers, employed or to be employed by the said *John Brown*, about the said Works; and the Commissioners for executing of this Act are hereby empowered for to ascertain the Quantity and Rates of the said Lands that shall be necessary for the said *Brown*, his Clerks, Dwellers, Work-men and Labourers to be employed about the said Works respectively, as aforesaid, and to order and appoint such Rents to be paid yearly to the ancient Proprietors and their Heirs, by the said *John Brown* and his Heirs, out of the said Lands, as they shall think fit, regard first only being had to the intrinsical Value of the said Lands.

[§ 38.] And whereas *Martin Supple*, Esq. having been restored as an Innocent by the Commissioners for Execution of the said Acts of Settlement to the ancient Estate of his Ancestors in the Lands and Tenements of *Ightermurramore*, *Ightermurrabegg*, *Ballintoonduing*, *Ringlass*, *Ballinenirnaugh*, and other Lands in the Barony of *Imokelly*, and County of *Cork* ; after which Restitution, Suit or Contest being commenced or moved by *Roger* late Earl of *Ossory*, who pretended a Title to the said Lands under the late Usurped Powers; and whereas the said *Martin Supple*, not being able to withstand the Power of the said Earl, was necessitated to purchase his Peace and Quiet, by conveying or exchanging his said ancient Estate unto the said Earl, and to accept for the same the Lands of *Drommodimore*, *Drommadibegg*, *Parnahelly*, *Boughallane*, in the said Barony and County, which Lands were held by the said Earl under the Titles of the said Acts of Settlement and Explanation, or one of them, and therefore by this present Act are restorable to the ancient Proprietors thereof: Be it therefore enacted by the Authority aforesaid, That all Conveyances and Assurances made by the said *Martin Supple* to the said Earl of the said ancient Estate, or of any part thereof, be and are hereby annulled and made void to all Intents and Purposes whatsoever: And that the said *Martin Supple* be and is hereby restored to the said ancient Estate, and shall and may hold and enjoy the same, according to such Estate and Title as he had therein, before the said Conveyance and Exchange thereof, made subject, and liable to all Remainders, Uses, Trusts, Limitations, and all other Estates, Charges and Incumbrances, as the said Estate or Lands from the said *Martin Supple* is to be removed, were or ought to have been liable unto, any thing herein to the contrary notwithstanding.

[§ 39.] Provided always, and be it further enacted by the Authority aforesaid, That this Act or any thing therein contained, shall not be construed or judged to vest in your Majesty, or to bar any Remainder or Remainders limited to Colonel *Richard Butler*, or to any of his Sons, upon the respective particular Estates limited to *James* Duke of *Ormond* and his Brother, in and of the ancient Estate, which on the 21st day of *October*, 1641, did rightfully belong unto *James* late Duke of *Ormond* deceased, or the Lady Dutchess his Wife, and the same to be subject to all Incumbrances whereunto the same ought to be liable, in case this Act were never made. Provided always, That the Remainder so limited to the said Colonel *Richard Butler* and his Sons, be such as is not, or was not in the Power of the said *James* now Duke of *Ormond*, and of his said Brother, or of either of them, to bar.

[§ 40.] And be it further enacted by the Authority aforesaid, and it is hereby declared to be the true intent and meaning of this Act, That all Lands, Tenements and Hereditaments, Uses, Trusts, Possession, Reversion or Remainder, Chattel real, and all and every other Estate, either in Law or Equity, of what nature or kind soever within this Kingdom, which on the said first Day of *August*, 1688, or at any time since did belong or appertain to the Society, Governors and Assistants of *London*, of the new Plantation of *Ulster* in the Kingdom of *Ireland*, or to any other Body Politick or Corporate, derived unto them, or composed or consisting of any the Citizens of *London*, by whatsoever Name or Names the same or any of them are called, be and are hereby vested in your Majesty, your Heirs and Successors, as from the first Day of *August*, 1688, and to be part of the Stock of Reprizals herein before mentioned, saving always the Right, Title, Estate and Interest of the Corporation of the

Mayor, Commons and Citizens of *London-Derry* and *Colerain*.

[§ 41.] And whereas several wast Plots of Ground within several Cities, Towns and Burroughs, or the Suburbs thereof within this Kingdom, at the publick Charges of the several Free holders and Inhabitants of the several and respective Counties, Cities, Towns and Burroughs, have been purchased from the then Proprietors, or reputed Proprietors thereof, and great Sums of Money laid out and expended by them in building of Session Houses, Gaols, Houses of Correction, and other public conveniences thereunto belonging, upon the said wast Plots of Ground, for the publick Good and Advantage of this Kingdom: And whereas the said wast Plots of Ground, or some of them so purchased and improved upon, may by this present Act, to the great Prejudice of this Commonwealth, be restored unto the old Proprietors thereof, if not by some special Clause or Proviso prevented: Be it therefore enacted by the Authority aforesaid, and it is hereby enacted, That all the Lands, Tenements, and Hereditaments so purchased as aforesaid, and whereupon any Session-Houses, Gaols, Houses of Correction are built, shall be and are hereby vested in your Majesty, your Heirs and Successors, to the Use herein after expressed; and that the several and respective old Proprietors of the said wast Plots of Ground shall by the Commissioners for Execution of this Act be forthwith reprized for the same out of some of the forfeited Lands vested in your Majesty, your Heirs and Successors by vertue of this Act, of equal Value, Worth and Purchase with the said wast Plots of Ground, before any Buildings or Improvements made thereupon, to have and to hold the said Lands to be set out in Reprizals, and them and every of them, their Heirs and Assigns, at or under the same, or like Tenures, Rents and Services, as all Purchasers are to hold by this Act, the Reprizals set out to them, or any of them, any thing in this present Act, or any other matter or thing to the contrary thereof in any wise notwithstanding

[§ 42.] Provided always, and it is hereby declared, That such of the waste Plots so built upon, as did not formerly belong unto and was the consecrated Ground or Site, Circuit, and Ambits of any Monastery, Abby, or other Religious House, shall be and remain vested in your Majesty, your Heirs and Successors, to the said publick Uses for which the same were so purchased and built upon: And as to all such of the said wast Plots so built upon as did formerly belong to, and was the consecrated Ground or Site, Circuit, and Ambits of any Monastery, Abby, or other Religious House, the same shall be and remain vested in your Majesty, your Heirs and Successors, to be disposed of to such pious or charitable Uses as your Majesty, your Heirs and Successors, shall think fit:

[§ 43.] And whereas some meriting Persons, who are to lose considerable Estates by this Act, might by the foregoing Rules be entituled to small or no Reprizals, but by their eminent Services may in a special manner merit your Majesty's Grace and Favour: Be it enacted by the Authority aforesaid, That your Majesty may in such special Cases set forth and grant Reprizals to such meriting Persons, as by your Majesty's Letters, under your Majesty's Privy Signet or Sign Manual, order the Commissioners for executing this Act to set forth Reprizals for them; and likewise, if your Majesty shall so think fit, to appoint and ascertain where and what Lands shall be set out to them.

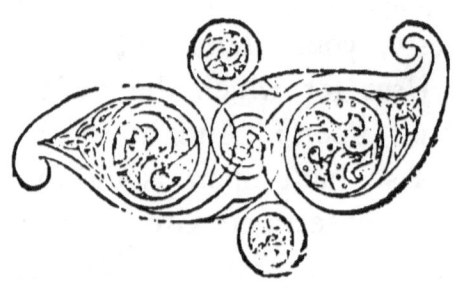

# CHAPTER VI.

## THE ACT OF ATTAINDER.

### CHAPTER XXX.

*An Act for the attainder of various rebels, and for pre͞ serving the interests of loyal subjects.*

THE authenticity of this act as printed by Archbishop King, has been questioned, especially by William Todd Jones in 1793. But we believe its authenticity cannot be successfully contested. Lesley, in his "Reply" to King, makes no attempt to disprove its existence, but, on the contrary, alludes to it and applauds James for having opposed it. King, however, asserts that the act was kept a secret; and that the persons attainted, or their friends, could not obtain a copy of it.\* For this Jones answers :

"But the fact (as stated by King) is impossible : conceive the absurdity ; an act of parliament is *smuggled*, where ! through two houses of lords and commons; of whom were they composed ? of catholics crowded with protestants ; though Leland, upon the authority of King, says there were but fourteen *real* protestants. Well, what did these two houses do ? They voted and passed a *secret* act of attainder of 2,500 protestants, which was to lie-by

\* The reason alleged by King for this course is that the existence of the Act might be denied in England. "State," &c., iii. 12, 18, 2. T. W. R

privately in petto, to be brought forward *at a proper time*; unknown, unheard of, by all the protestant part of the kingdom, till *peace* was restored: and that, according to King, was to be deemed *the proper time* for a renewal of *war* and *devastion*, by its publication and execution, and the secret was to be closely kept from nearly 3,000 persons, by the whole house of commons; by fifty-six peers, including primate Boyle, Barry lord Barrymore, Angier lord Longford, Forbes, the incomparable lord Granard (of whom more in my next continuation), Parsons lord Ross, Dopping bp. of Meath, Otway, bp. of Ossory, Wetenhal, bishop of Cork, Digby, bishop of Limerick, Bermingham lord Athenry, St. Lawrence lord Howth, Mallon lord Glenmallon, Hamilton lord Strabane, all protestants and many of them presbyterians, or rather puritans. It was kept close from 3,000 persons by all the privy council; by all the clerks of parliament who **engross and tack together bills**, it was to be kept an entire secret from all the protestants without doors, by all the protestants within the gates of parliament; and this probable, wise politic expectation was entertained *by those Catholic peers and representatives*, who through the cloud of war, passion, and uncertainty, could exercise the more than human moderation in solemnly prescribing the narrow bounds of thirty-eight years to all enquirers after titles under the revived court of claims: by those peers and representatives, whose patriotism, political knowledge, and comprehensive minds instructed them TO DECLARE THE INDEPENDENCE OF THE REALM, THE FREEDOM OF IRISH TRADE, AND THE INESTIMABLE VALUE OF A MARINE.—Good God, that any man, woman I mean, after such ACKNOWLEDGED, UNCONTROVERTED DOCUMENTS of the wisdom and reach of mind of that parliament, could be induced to credit and to advance the forgeries of a vicar of Bray under a persecuting protestant administration, FOR THE WICKED PURPOSE OF CALUMNIATING THEIR MEMORY, AND DEFEATING THE EFFORTS OF THEIR POSTERITY FOR FREEDOM. . . . . .

"A secret conspiracy BY WAY OF STATUTE against the lives of near three thousand people, appears in itself impracticable and

THE ACT OF ATTAINDER. 127

fabulous ; but that it should have been agitated IN OPEN PARLIA-
MENT, and in the hearing of the protestant members, and yet
expected to have been kept a secret from the protestants, *by these
protestant Members*, is childish and ridiculous.—In that parliament
sat the venerable lord Granard, a protestant, and *a constant ad-
herent and companion* of King James in Ireland—' This excellent
nobleman had married a lady of presbyterian principles ; was
protector of the northern puritans ; had humanely secreted their
teachers from those severities which in England proved both
odious and impolitic ; and had gained them an annual pension
of £500 from government.'—(Leland, vol. 3, p. 490.)—' It was
this lord Granard to whom the assembled protestants of Ulster,
by colonel Hamilton of Tullymore, who was sent to Dublin for
the sole purpose, unanimously offered the command of their
armed association, from their confidence in his protestant principles ; but he told Mr. Hamilton, THAT HE HAD LIVED
LOYAL ALL HIS LIFE, AND WOULD NOT DEPART FROM IT IN
HIS OLD AGE ; AND HE WAS RESOLVED THAT NO MAN SHOULD
WRITE REBEL UPON HIS GRAVESTONE.' (Lesley's "Reply,"
pp. 79, 80.) . . . . Is it then likely that this man would
be privy to a general protestant proscription, and not reveal
it ?—and is it probable that such a SECRET CONSPIRACY BY
WAY OF STATUTE could pass the houses of commons, and
lords, the privy council, and finally the King, and that it never
should come to the knowledge of a peer of parliament, a favourite
of the court, a resident in Dublin, and every day attendant in
his place in the upper house?"

The intrinsic improbability is well proved here, and
would suffice to show King's falsehood as to the secrecy
of the act; but if further proof were needed, the
authorities which prove the authenticity of the
act, utterly disprove the secrecy alleged by King.
The act is well described, in the London Gazette of July
1 to 4, 1689, and the names are given in print, in a

pamphlet licensed in London, the 2d day of the year 1690 (March 26th, old style).

Jones's statement as to the destruction of all papers relating to that parliament having been ordered, under a penalty of £500 and incapacity from office, is certain, and we give the clause in our note;* but this

* The clause for the destruction of the Records of the parliament of 1689, is in an act annulling the attainders and all acts of 1689.

"Be it enacted by the King's most excellent Majesty, by and with the advice and consent of the lords spiritual and temporal and commons in this present Parliament assembled, and by the authority of the same, That all and every the acts, or pretended acts, and the rolls whereon the said acts or pretended acts, and every of them, are recorded or engrossed, and all proceedings of what nature or kind soever had, made, done, or passed by the said persons lately so assembled at Dublin, pretending to be or calling themselves by the name of a Parliament, and also all writs issued in order to the calling of the said pretended Parliament, and returned into any office in this kingdom, and there remaining, and all the journals of the said pretended Parliament, and other books or writings in any wise relating thereunto, or to the holding thereof, shall, by the officers or persons in whose custody the same are, be brought before the lord deputy, or other chief governour or governours of this kingdom for the time being, at such time as the lord deputy, or other chief governour or governours for the time being shall appoint, at the council chamber in Dublin, and there shall be publickly and openly cancelled and utterly destroyed: and in case any officer or person in whose hands or custody the said acts and rolls, or proceedings, or any of them, do or shall remain, shall wilfully neglect or refuse to produce the same, to the intent that the same may be cancelled and destroyed, according to the true intent of this act, every such person and officer shall be, and is hereby adjudged and declared to be from clause was not enacted till 1695, and therefore could not have affected the acts of 1689, when King wrote in 1690.

Moreover, we cannot find any trace of Richard Darling (who professedly made the "*copia vera*" for King) as clerk in the office of the Master of the Rolls, or in any office, in 1690. A Richard Darling was appointed secretary to the commissioners for the inspection of forfeitures, by patent dated the 1st of June, 5 William III. (1693).

There certainly are grounds for supposing that some great jugglery, either as to the clauses or names in the act, was perpetrated by this well-paid and unscrupulous Williamite. The temptation to fabricate as much of the act (clauses or names) as possible, was immense. The want of scruple to commit any fraud is plain upon King's whole book. The likelihood of discovery alone would deter him. Probably every family who had a near relative in the "list," would be secured to William's interest, and no part of King's work could have helped more than this act to make that book what Burnet called it, " the best fitted to *settle* the minds " of the people of England, of any of the books published on the Revolution.

thenceforth incapable of any office or employment whatsoever and shall forfeit and pay the sum of five hundred pounds, one half thereof to his Majesty, and the other half to such person or persons that shall sue for the same by any action of debt, bill, plaint, or information, in any court of record whatsoever."— 7 *Will. III. Ir. c.* 1.

"*It is possible* an outline of some such bill might have been prepared by one of those hot-headed people of whom James had too many in his councils either for his safety or for his reputation, and they were chiefly ENGLISH; and that such draft of a bill having been laid before *parliament*, that wise, patriotic and sagacious *body* did meliorate and reduce it into 'the statute for the revival of the court of claims;' a law so unparalleled from its moderation in its review of forfeitures, by going back to *Cromwell's debentures exclusively*; a period of only thirty-eight years anterior to the date of their then sitting.

"Such a *draft of a bill*, like our own protestant bill for the castration of Romish priests, *which did pass* here but was cushioned in England,\* or like the *threat of a bill for levelling popish chapels*, which I myself heard made when I sat in the house of commons, such a draft of a bill, I say, might have been found among the baggage of the Duke of Tyrconnel, of Sir Richard Nagle, or of the unfortunate sovereign himself, for Burnet acquaints us, That all Tyrconnel's papers were taken in the camp; and those of James were found in Dublin. (Burnet's "Own Times," Vol. 2d, p. 30)."

The preamble states truly the rebellion of the northerns to dethrone their legitimate king, and bring in the Prince of Orange; and that the insurgents, though offered full pardon in repeated proclamations, still continued in rebellion. It enacts that certain persons therein named, who had "notoriously joyned in the said rebellion and *invasion*," or been slain in rebellion,

\* This is not quite correct. The penalty in the Bill, as it passed the Irish House of Commons, was branding on the cheek. In sending the Bill on to England the Irish Privy Council substituted castration. The English Government restored the original penalty. The Bill ultimately fell through, but not, it would seem, on this point. See Lecky, "History of England," Vol. I., ch. ii. T. W. R.

should be attainted of high treason, and suffer its penalties, *unless before the* 10*th of August following* (*i.e.* at least seven weeks from the passing of the act) they came and stood their trial for treason, according to law, when if otherwise acquitted, the act should not harm them. The number of persons in this clause vary in the different lists from 1270 to 1296.

It cannot be questioned that the persons here *conditionally* attainted, were in arms to dethrone the hereditary sovereign, supported, as he was, by a regularly elected parliament, by a large army, by foreign alliances, and by the good will of five-sixths of the people of Ireland. King he was *de jure* and *de facto*, and they sought to dethrone him, and to put a foreign prince on the throne. If ever there were rebels, they were.

As to their creed, there is no allusion to it. Roman Catholic and Protestant persons occur through the lists with common penalties denounced against both ; but neither creed is named in it.

We do not say whether those attainted were right or wrong in their rebellion : but the certainty that they were rebels according to the law, constitution, and custom of this and most other nations, justified the Irish parliament in treating them as such ; and should make all who sympathise with *these* rebels, pause ere they condemn every other party on whom law or defeat have fixed that name. Yet even this attaint is but *conditional ;* the parties had over seven weeks to surrender and take their trial, and the king could, at any time, for over four months after, grant them a pardon both as to persons and property—a pardon which, whether we consider his necessities and policy, his habitual leniency, or the repeated attempts to win back his rebellious subjects by the offer of free pardon, we believe he would have refused to few. This, too, is certain, that it *has never been even alleged that one single person suffered death under this much talked of act.* Of the constitutional character of the act, more presently.

The second article attaints persons who had absented themselves " since or shortly before " the 5th November, 1688, unless they return before the 1st of September, that is, in about ten weeks. Staying in England certainly looked like adhesion to the invader, yet the mere difficulty of coming over during the war should surely have been considered.

The third attaint is of persons absent before (some time probably before) 5th November, 1688, unless they return before the 1st October, that is, within about fourteen weeks.

Moreover, a certain number of the persons named in this conditional attaint are excepted from it specially, by a following clause, unless the king should go to England (their usual residence) before 1st October, 1689, and that after his arrival they should neglect to signify their loyalty to the satisfaction of his Majesty.

Yet Harris and "The List" licensed 26th March, 1690, have the audacity to *add* these English residents and make another list of attainted persons, *instead of deducting* them from the list under clause 3.

With similar want of faith, both these writers make out a fifth list of attaints of the persons explicitly not attainted, but whose *rents* are forfeited by sec. 8, so long as they continue absentees. Thus, two out of the five lists, by adding which Harris makes up his 2461 attaints, are not lists of attainders at all, and one of them should be rather deducted from one of the three lists of real attaints. Harris has under this exception for English residents, 547 names (though printed 647 in totting), and were we to deduct these and the fifth list of 85 persons, his number of attaints would fall to 1829; though he himself confesses that there must be some small drawback for persons attainted twice under different descriptions; and though his own totting, without removing either the fourth or fifth list, is only 2461, yet in his text he says, "about 2600" were attainted.

Yet Harris and "The List" pamphlet, which give the names in schedules, were more likely to misplace the lists than King, and he certainly did so in reference to the fourth list.

|   | Names. |
|---|---|
| King's first list, like the rest, contains | 1280 |
| His second, | 455 |
| And his third, | 197 |
|   | 1932 |
| And deducting the names in list 4, | 59 |
| King's list falls to | 1873 |

Yet even in this many are attainted twice over.

Harris's second list, and "The List's" third list each of 79 names, should be under title 4, namely, English residents, containing 59 in King. Harris's third list of 454 names should be second, namely, Absentees since 5th November, containing in King 455, and in "The List" 480 names. Harris's fourth list of 547, and "The List's" fourth list of 528 names should go to No. 3 in King, containing only 197 names, viz. of persons absent before 5th November. Without making these corrections, we would have the conditional attaints, under clauses 1, 2, and 3, amount in "The List" to 1311, in Harris to 1282, and in King to 1873. But if we make these corrections, King's will remain at 1873, Harris's rise to 2218, and "The List" to 2209.

It would, we think, puzzle La Place to calculate the probability of any particular name being authentic amid this wildernesss of inaccuracies.

The fifth class of 85 persons are, as we said, *not attainted at all.* The 8th section declares them to be absent from nonage, infirmity, &c., and denounces no penalty against their persons, but "it being much to the weakening and impoverishing of this Realm, that any of the Rents or profits of the Lands, Tenements, or Hereditaments thereof should be sent into or spent in any other place beyond the seas, but that the same should be kept and employed within the Realm for the better support and defence thereof," it vests the properties of these absentees in the King, until such time as these absentees return and apply by petition to the Chancery or Exchequer for their restoration. Harder penalties for absenteeism were enacted repeatedly before, and considering the necessities of Ireland in that awful struggle, this provision seems just, mild, and proper.*

By the fourth section, all the goods and properties of *all* the first four classes of absentees were also vested in the King till their return, acquittal, pardon or discharge. By the 5th and 6th sections, remainders and reversions to innocent persons after any estate for lives forfeited by the Act, are saved and preserved, provided (by the 7th section) claims to them are made within 60 days after the first sitting of the Court of Claims under the Act. But remainders in settlements, of which the uses could be changed, or where the lands were "plantation" lands, &c., were not saved. Whether such a Court of Claims ever sat is at least doubtful.

By the 9th and 11th sections, the rights and incumbrances of non-forfeiting persons over the forfeited estates are saved, provided (by section 12) their claims are made, as in case of remainder-men, &c.

* Lord Macaulay and after him Mr. T. D. Ingram press very severely against the Irish Parliament the charge that they attainted persons who were in many cases physically unable to accept the alternative offered them of a trial at law. The aim of the 8th section is to provide an easy remedy for persons who through no fault of their own might be prevented from surrendering themselves before the expiration of the term of grace. T. W. R.

The 10th section makes void Lord Strafford's abominable "offices," or confiscations of Connaught, Clare, Limerick, and Tipperary, and confirms the titles of the right owners, as if these offices had not been found.

The 13th section repeals a private act for conferring vast estates on Lord Albemarle out of the forfeitures on the Restoration.

The remaining clauses, except the last, have nothing to do with the Attainders. They are subsidiary to the Act repealing the Acts of Settlement and Explanation. They reprize ancient proprietors, who had bought or taken leases of their own estates from the owners under the Settlement Acts.

The 17th section provides for the completion of the Down or Strafford Survey, and for the reduction of excessive quit rents. In this section the phrase occurs, "their Majesties," but this is probably a mistake in printing, though a crotchety reasoner might find in it a doubt of the authenticity of the Act.

[The 21st and last section provides that any of the persons attainted "who shall return to their duty and loyalty" may be pardoned by royal warrant, provided that such pardon be issued "before the first day of November next, otherwise the pardon to be of no effect." T. W. R.]

## CHAPTER VII.

### CONCLUSION.

LET us now run our eyes over the deeds of the Feis, or Parliament of 1689. It came into power at the end of a half century of which the beginning was a civil and religious, social and proprietal persecution, combining all the atrocities to which Ireland had been alternately subject for four centuries and a half. Of this, the next stage was a partial insurrection, rendered universal by a bloody and rapacious government. The next stage was a war, in which civil and religious quarrels were so fiendishly combined, that it could not end while there was any one to fight with; in which the royalist dignitaries were the cruelest foes of the royalist armies and people, and in which the services done by cool and patriot soldiers were rendered useless by factious theologians. The next stage was conquest, slaughter, exile, confiscation, and the repose of solitude or of slavery. The next was a Restoration which gave back its worst prerogatives to the crown, but gave the restorers and royalists only a skirt of their properties. Then came a struggle for proprietal justice and religious toleration, met by an infamous conspiracy of the deceptious aristocracy and the fanatic people of England, to blast the characters of the Irish, and decimate the men; and lastly, a king, who strained his prerogative to do them justice, is driven from England by a Dutchman, supported by blue guards, black guards, and flaming lies, and is forced to throw himself on the generosity and prudence of Ireland.

A faction existed who raised a civil war in every province; and in every province, save one, it was suppressed; but in that one it continued, and the sails of an invading fleet already flap in the Channel breeze when this parliament is summoned.

How difficult was their position! How could they act as freemen, without appearing ungenerous to a refugee and benefactor king? How guard their nationality, without quarrelling with him or alienating England from him? How could they do that proprietal justice and grant that religious liberty for which the country had been struggling? How check civil war—how sustain a war by the resources of a distracted country? Yet all this the Irish parliament did, and more too; for they established the principal parts of a code needful for the *permanent* liberty and prosperity of Ireland.

Take up the list of acts passed in their session of seventy-two days, and run over them. They begin by recognising their lawful king who had thrown himself among them. They pledge themselves to him against his powerful foe. Knowing full well the struggle that was before them, and that lukewarm and malcontent agents might ruin them, they tossed aside those official claims, which in times of peace and safety should be sacred.

But their next act deserves more notice. It must not be forgotten that Molyneux's "Case of Ireland," which the parliaments of England and Ireland first burnt, and ended by declaring and enacting as sound law, was published in 1699, just ten years after this parliament of James's. Doubtless the antique rights of the native Irish, the comparative independence of the Pale, the arguments of Darcy, the memory of the council of Kilkenny, might suggest to Molyneux those principles of independence, which one of his cast of mind would hardly reach by general reasoning. But why go so far back, and to so much less apt precedents? Here, in the parliament of 1689, was a law made declaring Ireland to be and to have always been a "distinct kingdom" from England; "always governed by his majesty and his predecessors according to the ancient customs, laws, and statutes thereof, and that the parliament of Ireland, and that *alone*, could make laws to bind this kingdom;" and expressly enacting and declaring that no law save such as the Irish parliament might make should bind Ireland. And this act prohibited all English jurisdiction in Ireland, and all appeals to the English peers or to any other court out of Ireland. Is not this the whole argument of Molyneux, the hope of Swift and Lucas, the attempt of Flood, the achievement of Grattan and the Volunteers? Is not this an epitome of the Protestant patriot attempts, from the Revolution to the Dungannon Convention? Is not this the soul of '82? Surely if it be, as it is, just to track the stream of liberation back to Molyneux, we should not stop there; but when we find that a parliament which sat only ten years before his book was published, which must have been a daily subject of conversation,—as it certainly was of written polemics—during those ten years; when we find this upper fountain so obviously streaming into the thought of Molyneux, should we not associate the parliament of 1689 with that of 1782, and place Nagle and Rice and its other ruling spirits along with Flood and Grattan in our gratitude?

Moreover, the lords and commons expressly repealed Poyning's law, and passed a bill creating Irish Inns of Court, and abolishing the rules for keeping terms in London. But the king rejected these. We are to this day without this benefit which the senate of '89 tried to give us; and the future advocates and judges of Ireland are hauled off to a foreign and dissolute capital to go through an idle and expensive ceremony, term after term, as an essential to being allowed to practice in the courts of this their native kingdom.

The Act (c. 4.) for restoring the ancient gentry to their possessions, we have already canvassed. It were monstrous to suppose the parliament ought to have respected the thirty-eight years' usurpation of savage invaders, and to have overlooked the rights of the national chieftains, the plundered proprietors who lived, and whose families lived, to claim their rights. The care with which purchasers and incumbrancers were to be reprized we have already noticed; yet we cannot but repeat our regret, that the bill of the Lords (which left the adventurers of Cromwell a moiety of their usurpations) did not pass.

Naturally related to this are the Acts, c. 24, for vesting attainted absentees' goods in the King, and c. 30, attainting a number of insurgents. We have already shown from King, that the Whigs had taken good care of the two things forfeited—their chattels, which they had sent to them, without opposition, during the month of March, and their persons, which they put under the guard of the gallant insurgents of Derry and Fermanagh, or in the keeping of William and the charity of England. How poorly they were treated then in England, may be guessed at by the choice men of the impoverished defenders of Derry having been left without money, aye, or even clothing or food in the streets of London.

We heartily censure this Attainder Act. It was *the* mistake of the Irish Parliament. It bound up the hearts and interests of those who were named in it, and of their children, in William's success. It could not be enforced: they were absent. It could not be terrible till victory sanctioned it, and then it would be needless and cruel to execute. Yet, let us judge the men rightly. James had been hunted out of England by lies, treachery, bigotry, cabal, and a Dutch invader, for having attempted to grant religious liberty by his prerogative. Those attainted were, nine out of ten, in arms against him and their country. They had been repeatedly offered free pardon. Just before the act was brought in, a free pardon, excepting only ten persons, was offered, yet few of the insurgents came in; and James, instead of forbidding quarter, or hanging his prisoners, or any other of the acts of rigour usual in hereditary governments down to our own time, consented to an act requiring the chief persons of the insurrection to come, in periods specified, and amply long enough to stand their trials. Certain it is, as we said before, that though many of these were or became prisoners, none were executed. The act was a dead letter; and considering the principles of the time, surely the act was not wonderful.

In order, then, to judge them better, let us see what the other side—the immaculate Whigs, who assailed the Irish—did when they were in power. Of anything previous to the Revolution—of the treachery and blood, by law and without law, under the Plantagenets, Tudors, Stuarts, and the Commonwealth, 'tis needless to speak. But let us see what their neighbours, the Williamites, did.

The Irish Attainder Act was not brought in till the

end of June. Now, this is of great value, for the dates of the last papers on Ireland, laid before the English Commons, having been 10th June, 1689, they, on the 20th June, "*Resolved*, that leave be given to bring in a Bill, to attaint of high treason certain persons who are now in Ireland, or any other parts beyond the seas, adhearing to their Majesties' enemies, and shall not return into England by a certain day." *

* The dates about the time of this revolution are most important. On the 10th October, 1688, William issued an address, dated at the Hague, and another from the same place, dated 24th October, intended to counterwork James's retractations. He landed at Torbay, November 5th, arrived in London December 17th. Some Whig Lords signed an association, dated December 19th, pledging themselves to stand by the prince, and avenge him if he should perish. December 23d, William issued the letter calling the members of Charles II.'s parliament, the mayor, alderman, and 50 councillors of London. December 26th, they met, called on the prince to assume the government and issue letters for a convention, and they signed the association of the Whig Lords. They presented their address 27th December, it was received December 28th, and then this little club broke up. December 29th, William issued letters for a convention, which met 22d January, 1688-9, finally agreed on their declaration against James and his family, and for William and Mary, 12th February ; and these, king and queen, were proclaimed 13th February, 1688-9. February 19th, a Bill was brought in to call the convention a parliament ; it passed, and received royal assent 23d February. By this the lords and gentlemen who met 22d January, were named the two houses of parliament, and the acts of this convention-parliament were to date from 13th February. This hybrid sat till 20th August, and having passed the Attainder Act, was adjourned to 20th September, and then 19th October, 1689.

The very next entry is—"A Bill for the attainting certain persons of high treason, was read the first time." "*Resolved*, that the Bill be read a second time."

Here was a bill to attaint persons beyond seas in another kingdom where William had never been acknowledged—where James was welcomed by nine men out of ten—from whence, so far from being able to procure evidence or allow defence, they could but by accident get intelligence and reports once in some months. It is not here pretended that the attainted were habitual residents in England. The bill passed the second reading and was committed, June 22d, with an instruction to the committee, "That they insert into the bill such other of the persons as were this day *named in the house*, as they shall find cause."

Again, on the 24th—"*Ordered*, that it be an instruction to the committee, to whom the bill for attainting certain persons is referred, that they prepare and bring in a clause for the *immediate* seizing the estates of such persons who are *or* shall be proved to be in arms with the late King James in Ireland, or in his service in France." On the 29th is another instruction to "prepare and bring in a clause, that the estates

---

This second session lasted till 27th January, 1689-90, when it was stopped by a prorogation to the 2d April; but before that day it was dissolved, and a parliament summoned by writ, which met 20th March, 1689, and as a first law, passed an act ratifying the proceedings of the convention.

of the persons who are now in rebellion (!) in Ireland be applied to the relief of the Irish Protestants fled into this realm; and also to declare all the proceedings of the pretended parliament and courts of justice, now held in Ireland, to be null and void;" the committee "to sit *de die in diem*, till the bill be finished."

Up to this time they could not have known that any attainder act had been brought in in Ireland. On the 9th July, Sergeant Trenchard reported, "That the committee had *proof*" (we shall presently see of what kind) " of *several other* persons being in Ireland in arms with King James, and therefore had agreed their names should be inserted in the bill." " Ordered, that the bill, so amended, be engrossed." On the 11th July the bill passed, inserting *August*, 1689, in stead of August next, and inserting some Christian names.

The bill reached the Lords.

Upon the 24th July a message was sent to the Lords, urging the despatch of the bill. On the 2nd August, at a conference, the Lords required to know *on what evidence* the names were introduced as being in Ireland, "for, upon their best inquiry, they say they cannot learn some of them have been there—they instanced the Lord Hunsden." On the 3d of August, Mr. Sergeant Trenchard acquaints the house, that the names of those who gave evidence at the bar of the house, touching the persons who are named in the bill of attainder, being in Ireland, were Bazill Purefoy and William Dalton; and those at the committee, to whom the bill was referred, were William Watts and Math. Gun;" four persons, two and two giving the whole evidence for the attainder of those who stood by King James in Ireland! This report was handed to the Lords on the 5th August.

On the 20th August the Lords returned the bill, with some amendments, leaving out Lord Hunsden and four or five more, and inserting a few others; and upon this day the parliament was prorogued.

Again, on the 30th October, a bill was ordered to attaint all such persons as were in rebellion against their Majesties. On the 26th November, certain members were ordered to prepare a bill attainting all who had been in arms against William and Mary, since 14*th February*, 1688-9, or any time since, and all who *have been*, or shall be, *aiding, assisting, or abetting* them. On the 10th December the bill was reported and read a first time, and the committee ordered to bring in a bill for sale of the estates forfeited thereby.

On the 4th April, 1690, another bill was ordered, and was read 22d April.

Again, on 22d October, another attainder and confiscation bill was brought and passed the Commons, on the 23d December.

Wearied at length by unsuccessful bills, which the better or more interested feeling of the Lords, or the policy of the King, perpetually defeated, they abandoned any further attainder bills, and merely advertized for money on the forfeited lands in Ireland.

The attainders in *court* might satisfy them. The commissioners of forfeitures, under 10 William III., c. 9, reported to the Commons on the 15th of December, 1699, that the persons outlawed for treason in Ireland since the 13th of February, 1688-9, on account of the late rebellion, were 3921 in number. It was abominable for James's parliament to attaint conditionally the rebels against the old king, but reasonable for the Whigs to attaint about double the number absolutely, for never having recognized the new king! These 3921 had properties, says the report, to the amount of 1,060,792 *plantation* acres, worth £211,623 a year, and worth in money £2,685,130, "besides the several denominations in the said several counties to which no number of acres can be added, by reason of the imperfection of the surveys not here valued." Of these 3921, there were 491 restored under the first commission on the articles of Galway and Limerick; and 792 under the second commission, having joint properties of 233,106 acres, worth £55,763 a year, or £724,923 purchase, leaving 2638 persons, having 827,686 acres, worth £155,859 a year, or £1,960,206. Yet the fees were monstrous, say the commissioners, in these Courts of Claims, £5 being the register's fees for even *entering* a claim. William restored property to the amount of 74,733 acres, worth £20,066 per annum, or £260,863 in all, which would leave as absolutely forfeited property, 752,953 acres, worth £135,793 a year, and

£1,699,343 in all; and even were we to deduct in proportion, which we ought not, as those pardoned were chiefly the very wealthy few, there would remain over 2400 persons attained by office, after deducting all who carved out their acquittal with shot and sword, and all whom the tenderness or wisdom of the king pardoned.

The commissioners state that £300,000 worth of chattels were seized, not included in the above estimate; nor were 297 houses in Dublin, 26 in Cork, 226 elsewhere, mills, chief rents, £60,000 worth of woods, &c. in it.

Most of these properties had been given away freely by William. Amongst his grants they specify all King James's estates, over 95,000 acres, worth £25,995 a year, to Mrs. Elizabeth Villiers, Countess of Orkney. She was William's favourite mistress. James, to his honour be it spoken, had thrown these estates into the general fund for reprisal of the injured Irish.

Here then is, certainly not a justification of the parliament of 1689, in passing the attainder act, but evidence from the journals of the English parliament and the reports of their commissioners, that they tried to do worse than the Irish parliament (under far greater excuses) are accused of having done, and that the actual amount of punishment *inflicted* by the Williamite courts in Ireland, far exceeded what the Irish parliament of 1689 had *conditionally threatened.*

The next Acts as a class are c. 9, repealing ministers' money act; c. 12, granting perfect liberty of conscience to men of all creeds; c. 13, directing Roman Catholics to pay their tithes to their own priests; c. 14, on Ulster poundage; c. 15, appointing those tithes to the *parish* priests, and recognizing as a Roman Catholic prelate, no one but him whom the king under privy signet and sign manual should signify and recognize as such. All these acts went to create religious equality, certainly not the voluntary system; neither party approved of it then; but to make the Protestant support his own minister, and the Roman Catholic his own, without violation of conscience, or a shadow of supremacy. The low salaries (£100 to £200 a year) of the Roman Catholic prelates, and their exclusion from parliament, were in the same moderate spirit.

Again, this parliament introduced the statute of frauds, (which having been set aside, was not adopted until the 7th William III.;) acts for relief of poor debtors, for the speedy recovery of wages, and for ratifying wills and deeds by persons out of possession.

Chap. 21, forbidding the importation of foreign coals, was designed to render this country independent of English trade. At that time the bogs were larger and the people fewer. Their opinion that this importation, which " hindred the industry of several poor people and labourers, who might have employed themselves" in supplying the cities, &c. with turf, reminds us of Mr. Laing's most able notice in his "Norway," of the immense employment to men, women, and children by the cutting of fire-wood; and what a powerful means this is of doing that which is as important as the production of wealth, the diffusion of it without any great inequality through all classes. Part of c. 29, encouraging trade, laying heavy import duties on English goods, and giving privileges to Irish ships over foreign, especially over English, was the result of sound practical patriotism. It was necessary to guard our trade, manufactures, and shipping against the rivalry of a near, rich, and aspiring neighbour, that would crush them in their cradles. It was wise to raise the energies of infant adventure by favour, and not trust it in a reckless competition. The example, too, of all countries which had reared up commerce by their own favour and their neighbour's surrender of trade, would have justified them.

Besides the schools for the Navy under c. 29, c. 16 deals also with schools. We have not the latter Act; but, considering James's known zeal for education, his foundation of the Kilkenny college, and the spirit of the provision in c. 29, we may guess the liberality of the other. One of the most distinguished of our living historians has told us that he remembered having seen evidence that this Act established a school for general (national) education in every parish in Ireland.

C. 10, the Act of Supply; c. 25, Martial Law, and

CONCLUSION. 151

this Act, c. 29, were a code of defence. The supply was proportioned to their abilities: every exertion was made, and all efforts were needed. Plowden puts the effect of this c. 29 not ill :—-

"Although James were averse from passing the acts I have already mentioned, he probably encouraged another which passed *for the advance and improvement of trade and for encouragement and increase of shipping and navgiation*, which purported to throw open to Ireland a free and immediate trade with all our plantations and colonies ; to promote ship-building, by remitting to the owners of Irish built vessels, large proportions of the duties of custom and excise, encourage seamen by exempting them for ten years from taxes, and allowing them the freedom of any city or sea-port they should chuse to reside in, and improve the Irish navy by establishing free schools for teaching and instructing in the mathematics and the art of navigation, in Dublin, Belfast, Waterford, Cork, Limerick, and Galway. If James looked up to any probability of maintaining his ground in Ireland he must have been sensible of the necessity of an Irish navy. No man was better qualified to judge of the utility of such institutions than this prince. He was an able seaman, fond of his profession ; and to his industry and talent does the British navy owe many of its best signals and regulations. The firmness, resolution and enterprise which had distinguished him, whilst Duke of York, as a sea officer, abandoned him when king, both in the cabinet and the field."

Thus then this parliament exercised less severity than any of its time, it established liberty of conscience and equality of creeds, it proscribed no man for his religion—-the word Protestant does not occur in any act—(though, while it sat, the Westminster Convention was not only thundering out insults against "popery," but exciting William to persecute it, and laying the foundation of the penal code)—it introduced many laws of great practical value in the business of society, it removed the disabilities of the natives, the scars of old fetters; it was generous to the king, yet carried its own opinions out against his where they differed; it finally—and what should win the remembrance and veneration of Irishmen through all time—it boldly announced our national independence, in words which Molyneux shouted on to Swift, and Swift to Lucas, and Lucas to Flood, and Flood and Grattan redoubling the cry, Dungannon church rang, and Ireland was again a nation. Yet something it said escaped the hearing or surpassed the vigour of the last century; it said, "Irish commerce fostered," and it was faintly heard, but it said, "an Irish navy to shield our coasts," and it said, "an Irish army to scathe the invaders," and Grattan neglected both, and our coast had no guardian, and our desecrated fields knew no avenger.

We have printed the king's speech at the opening of this eventful parliament, the titles of *all* its acts, and all the statutes summarized in full detail which we could in any way procure—sufficient, we think, with the scattered notices of the chief members, to make the working of this parliament plain. We are conscious of many defects in our information and way of treating the subject; but we commenced by avowing that we were not professors but students of Irish history; trying to come at some clear understanding on a most important part of it, communicating our difficulties and offering our solutions, as they occurred to us, in hopes that some of our countrymen would take up the same study, and do as much or more than we had done, and possibly that one of those accomplished historians, of which Ireland now has a few, would take the helm from us, and guide the ship himself.

We have no reason to suppose that we succeeded in either object; yet we cling to the belief that, owing to us, some few persons will for the future be found, who will not allow the calumnies against our noble old parliament of 1689 to pass uncontradicted. It might have been better, but this is well.

# APPENDIX A.

*A LIST of the Lords Spiritual and Temporal who sate in the* Parliament *held in* Dublin, *in* 1689, *under the late King* James II.

[N.B.—In the following list, J. indicates the "Journal of the Proceedings of the Parliament in Ireland," (printed in London, July 6, 1689,) as the authority to show that the individual sat in the Parliament. T. indicates the "True Account :" K. indicates the appendix to Archbishop King's "State of the Protestants, &c." pp. 90, 91 : R. indicates Ebenezer Rider's "Appendix to the late King James's Acts," (Dublin, 1740) : H. indicates the "Appendix to Walter Harris's Life of William III." pp. 32, 33, (Dublin, 1749,) as the authority.]

### THE LORD PRIMATE.

Dr. Michael Boyle, Lord Archbishop of Armagh, Primate of all Ireland. [J. K.]

### THE LORD CHANCELLOR.

Sir Alexander Fitton, Knt. Lord Fitton and Lord Baron of Gosworth, in the County of Limerick, Lord High Chancellor of Ireland. [J. T. K. R. H.]

### DUKE.

Richard Talbot, Duke of Tyrconnell, [J. T. K. H.] Lord Lieutenant of Ireland, and Captain General of the Royal Forces in Ireland.

## APPENDIX.

### EARLS.

Richard Bourk, Earl of Clanrickard, [T. H.] Lord Lieutenant of Galway.

Alexander MacDonnel, Earl of Antrim, [T. K. II.] Lord Lieutenant of Antrim.

Richard Nugent, Earl of Westmeath, [T. K. R. H.] Lord Lieutenant of Westmeath.

Richard Nugent, Earl of Barrymore. [T. K. R. II.]

Richard Lambert, (spelled Lambart in Lodge's Peerage, Ed. 1754) Earl of Cavan. [K.]

Donogh MacCarthy, Earl of Clancarty. [T. K. R. II.]

Richard Poer, Earl of Tyrone, [T. K. R. H.] Lord Lieutenant of Waterford.

Francis Aungier, Earl of Longford. [T. K. R. II.]

Arthur Forbes, Earl of Granard. [J. T. K. R. II.]

William Dungan, Earl of Limerick, [T. K. R. II.] Lord Lieutenant of Kildare.

### VISCOUNTS.

Jenico Preston, Lord Viscount Gormanstown, [T. K. H.] Lord Lieutenant of Meath.

David Roche, Lord Viscount Fermoy. [T. II.]

Richard Butler, Lord Viscount Mountgarret. [T. K. R. II.]

Theobald Dillon, Lord Viscount Costello-Galen, Viscount Dillon, Lord Dillon, Lord Lieutenant of Roscommon.

Arthur Magennis, Lord Viscount Iveagh, [T. K. R. II.] Lord Lieutenant of Down.

Dominick Sarsfield, Lord Viscount Kilmallock. [T. K. R. II.]

Theobald Bourk, Lord Viscount Mayo. [K.]

Pierce Butler, Lord Viscount Ikerin. [K.]

Maximilian O'Dempsy, Lord Viscount Clanmalier, [T. R. H.] Lord Lieutenant of the Queen's County.

Pierce Butler, Lord Viscount Galmoy, [T. R. II.] Lord Lieutenant of Kilkenny.

Nicholas Barnewall, Lord Viscount Kingsland. [K.]

APPENDIX. 157

Daniel O'Brian, Lord Viscount Clare, [T. K. H.] Lord Lieutenant of Clare.
Richard Parsons, Lord Viscount Ross. [T. K. R. H.]
Ulick Bourk, Lord Viscount Galway. [T. K. R. H.]
Sir Valentine Browne, Lord Viscount Kinmare, Baron Castle Rosse, *lately made*, (24th July, 1784,) [T. K. R. H.] Lord Lieutenant of Kerry. ["Kilmore" (in King) is evidently a mistake for "Kinmare."]
Justin MacCarty, Lord Viscount Mount Cashel, Baron Castlehench, *lately made*, (25th May, 1789) [T. K. R. H.] Lord Lieutenant of Cork, Master General of the Ordnance.

BISHOPS.

Dr. Anthony Dopping, Lord Bishop of Meath. [J. T. K. R. H.]
Dr. Hugh Gore, Lord Bishop of Waterford and Lismore. [J.]
Dr. Thomas Otway, Lord Bishop of Ossory. [J. T. K. R. H.]
Dr. Edward Wettenhall, Lord Bishop of Cork and Ross. [J. T. K. R. H.]
Dr. Simon Digby, Lord Bishop of Limerick and Ardfert. [J. T. K. R. H.]

BARONS.

Edward Bermingham, Lord Baron of Athenry, [K. R.] Lord Lieutenant of Mayo.
Almericus Courcy, Lord Baron of Kinsale. [T. K. K. H.]
William Fitzmaurice, Lord Baron of Kerry and Lixnaw. [K.]
Thomas St. Lawrence, Lord Baron of Howth. [T. K. R. H.]
Christopher Fleming, Lord Baron of Slane. [T. K. R. H.]
Robert Barnewall, Lord Baron of Trimleston. [T. K. R. H.]
Christopher Plunket, Lord Baron of Dunsany. [T. K. R. H.]
Pierce Butler, Lord Baron of Dunboyne. [T. K. R. H.]
Brian Fitzpatrick, Lord Baron of Upper Ossory. [T. K. R. H.]
Matthew Plunket, Lord Baron of Louth, [K.] Lord Lieutenant of Louth.
William Bourk, Lord Baron of Castle-Connell. [T. K. H.]
Pierce Butler, Lord Baron of Cahir. [T. K. R. H.]

Theobald Bourk, Lord Baron of Brittas, [T. K. R. H.] Lord Lieutenant of Limerick.
Thomas Folliot, Lord Baron of Ballyshannon. [H.]
Henry Blaney, Lord Baron of Monaghan. [K.]
Dermot Malone, Lord Baron of Glenmalun and Courchey. [T. K. R. H.]
Connor Maguire, Lord Baron of Iniskillin, [T. K. R. H.] Lord Lieutenant of Fermanagh.
Claud Hamilton, Lord Baron of Strabane. {T. K. R. H.]
John Bellew, Lord Baron of Duleek. [T. K. H.]
Alexander Fitton, Baron of Gosworth, (1st April, 1689) [*vide* Chancellor.]
John Burke, Lord Baron of Bophin, *lately made*. (2nd April, 1689.) [J. T. K. R. H.]
Thomas Nugent, Lord Baron of Riverstown, *lately made*, (3rd April, 1689.) [T. K. R. H.]

*An exact LIST of the Knights, Citizens and Burgesses, who were returned and sate in the* Parliament *held in* Dublin *under the late King* James *in* 1689.

*Note. Those wanting are for* Londonderry, Inniskellin, *and such Places as were in the* Protestants' *Hands.*

## County of ANTRIM.

Cormac O'Neill, Esq. ;
Randal MacDonnell, Esq.

## Borough of *Belfast*.

Marcus Talbot, Esq. ;
Daniell O'Neill, Esq. ; returned 20th May, 1689.

## County of ARDMAGH.

Arthur Brownlow, Esq. ;
Walter Hovenden, Esq.

## Borough of *Ardmagh*.

Francis Stafford, Esq. ;
Constantine O'Neill, Esq. ; returned 20th May, 1689.

APPENDIX.

County of CATHERLAGH [Carlow].
Dudley Bagnal, Esq.;
Henry Lutterell, Esq.

Borough of *Catheriagh*
Marcus Baggot, Esq.;
John Warren, Esq.

Borough of *Old Leighlin*.
Darby Long, Esq.;
Daniel Doran, Esq.

County of CAVAN.
Philip Reilly, of Aghnecrevy, Esq.;
John Reilly, of Garirobuck, Esq.

Borough of *Cavan*.
Philip Og O'Reilly, Esq.;
Hugh Reilly, of Lara, Esq.

Borough of *Belturbet*.
Sir Edward Tyrrel, Bart.;
Philip Tuite, of Newcastle, Esq.

County of CLARE.
Daniel O'Brien, Esq.;
John Macnamara, of Crattlagh, Esq.

Borough of *Ennis*.
Florence Macnamara, of Dromad, Esq.; 10th May, 1689;
Theobald Butler, of Strathnagaloon, Esq.; 10th May, 1689.

County of CORK.
Justin MacCarthy, Esq.;
Sir Richard Nagle, Knight.

City of *Cork*.
Sir James Cotter, Knight;
John Galloway, Esq.

### Town of *Youghal.*
Thomas Uniack, Alderman;
Edward Gough, Alderman.

### Town of *Kinsale.*
Andrew Murrogh, Esq.;
Miles de Courcy, Esq.

### Town of *Bandon-bridge.*
Charles MacCarthy, of Ballea, Esq.;
Daniel MacCarthy Reagh, Esq.

### Town of *Mallow.*
John Barret, of Castlemore, Esq.;
David Nagle, of Carragowne, Esq.

### Borough of *Baltimore.*
Daniel O'Donovan, Esq.;
Jeremy Donovan, Esq.

### Borough of *Cloghnakilty.*
Lieutenant Colonel Owen MacCarthy;
Daniel [Mac] Fion MacCarthy, Esq.

### Borough of *Charleville.*
John Baggot, Sen. of Baggotstown, Esq.;
John Power, of Killballane, Esq.

### Borough of *Middleton.*
Dermot Long, Esq.;
John Long, Esq.

### Borough of *Rathcormac.*
James Barry, Esq.;
Edward Powel, Esq.

### Borough of *Doneraile.*
Daniel O'Donovan, Esq.;
John Baggot, Jun., of Baggotstown, Esq.

APPENDIX. 161

County of DOWN.

Murtagh MacGennis, of Green-Castle, Esq.;
Ever MacGennis, of Castle-Welan, Esq.

Borough of *Killeleagh*.

Bernard MacGennis, of Ballygorianbeg, Esq.;
Toole O'Neill, of Drummekelly, Gent.

Borough of *Newry*.

Rowland White, Esq.;
Rowland Savage, Esq.

County and Town of DROGHEDA.

Henry Dowdall, Esq.; Recorder;
Christopher Peppard Fitz-George, Alderman.

County of DUBLIN.

Simon Lutterel, of Lutterelstown, Esq.;
Patrick Sarsfield, jun., of Lucan, Esq.

City of *Dublin*.

Sir Michael Creagh, Knight, Lord Mayor;
Terence Dermot, Sen. Alderman.

University of *Dublin*.

Sir John Meade, Knight;
Joseph Coghlan, Esq.

Borough of *Swords*.

Francis Barnewell, of Woodpark, in the County of Meath, Esq.;
Robert Russel, of Drynham, Esq.

Borough of *Newcastle*.

Thomas Arthur, of Colganstown, Esq.;
John Talbot, of Belgard, Esq.

County of GALWAY.

Sir Ulick Bourk, Bart.;
Sir Walter Blake, Bart.

R

### Town of *Galway.*

Oliver Martin, Esq.;
John Kirwan, Esq.

### Town of *Athenry.*

James Talbot, of Mount-Talbot, Esq.;
Charles Daly, of Dunsandal, Esq.

### Borough of *Tuam.*

James Lally, of Tullendaly;
William Bourk, of Carrowfrila.

### County of KERRY.

Nicholas Brown, Esq.;
Sir Thomas Crosby, Knight.

### Borough of *Dingle-Icouch.*

Edward Rice Fitz-James, of Ballinelig in the County of Limrick, Esq.;
John Hussey, of Culmullin, Esq.

### Borough of *Tralee.*

Maurice Hussey, of Kerry, Esq.;
John Brown, of Ardagh, Esq.

### Borough of *Ardfert.*

Colonel Roger MacElligot, Esq.;
Cornelius MacGillicuddy, Esq.

### County of KILDARE.

John Wogan, Esq.;
George Aylmer, Esq.

### Borough of *Kildare.*

Francis Leigh, Esq.;
Robert Porter, Esq.

### Borough of *Naas.*

Walter Lord Dungan;
Charles White, Esq.

APPENDIX.

### Borough of *Athy.*
William Fitzgerald, Esq. ;
William Archbold, Esq.

### Borough of *Harrystown.*
James Nihel, Esq. ;
Edmond Fitzgerald, Esq.

### County of KILKENNY.
James Grace, of Courstown, Esq.;
Robert Walsh, of Cloneneassy, Esq.

### City of *Kilkenny.*
John Rooth, Mayor ;
James Bryan, Alderman ; 4th May, 1689.

### Borough of *Gowran.*
Richard Butler, Esq, ;
Colonel Robert Fielding, by a new election ;
Walter Kelly, Esq., Doctor of Physic.

### Borough of *Thomastown.*
Robert Grace, Sen., Esq. ;
Robert Grace, Jun., Esq.

### Borough of *Inistiog:.*
Edward Fitzgerald, Esq. ;
James Fitzgerald, Esq.

### Borough of *Callan.*
Walter Butler, Esq. ;
Thady Meagher, Esq.

### Borough of *Knocktopher.*
Harvey Morres, Esq. ;
Henry Meagh, Esq.

### KING'S COUNTY.
Hewer Oxburgh, Esq. ;
Owen Carroll, Esq.

### Borough of *Banaghar*.

Terence Coghlan, Esq. ;
Terence Coghlan, Gent.

### Borough of *Philipstown*.

John Connor, Esq. ;
Hewer Oxburgh, Esq.

### County of LEITRIM.

Edmond Reynells, Esq. ;
Iriel Farrel, Esq.

### Borough of *James-Town*

Alexander MacDonnel, Esq. ; 15th May, 689 ;
William Shanley, Esq. ; 15th May, 1689.

### County of LIMERICK.

Sir James Fitzgerald, Bart. ;
Gerald Fitzgerald, Knight of the Glyn.

### City of *Limerick*.

Nicholas Arthur, Alderman ;
Thomas Harrold, Alderman.

### Borough of *Killmallock*.

Sir William Harley, Bart. ;
John Lacy, Esq.

### Borough of *Askeyton*.

John Bourk, of Cahirmoyhill, Esq. ;
Edward Rice, Esq.

### County of LONGFORD.

Roger Farrell, Esq. ;
Robert Farrell, Esq.

### Borough of *Lanesborough*.

Oliver Fitzgerald, Esq. ;
Roger Farrell, Esq.

APPENDIX.

Borough of *St. Johnstown*.
Sir William Ellis, Knight;
Lieutenant Colonel James Nugent.

County of LOUTH.
Thomas Bellew, Esq. ;
William Talbot, Esq.

Borough of *Atherdee*.
Hugh Gernon, Esq.;
John Babe, Esq.

Borough of *Dundalk*.
Robert Dermot, Esq. ;
John Dowdgall, Esq.

Borough of *Carlingford*.
Christopher Peppard Fitz-Ignatius, Esq. ;
Bryan Dermot, Esq.

County of MAYO.
Gerald Moore, Esq. ;
Walter Bourk, Esq.

Borough of *Castlebar*.
John Bermingham, Esq., Portreeve ;
Thomas Bourk, Esq.

County of MEATH.
Sir William Talbot, Bart. ;
Sir Patrick Barnewall, Bart.

Borough of *Trim*.
Captain Nicholas Cusacke;
Walter Nangle, Esq.

Borough of *Athboy*.
John Trynder, Esq. ;
Robert Longfield, Esq.

### Borough of *Navan*.

Christopher Cusacke, of Corballis, Esq. ;
Christopher Cusacke, of Ratholeran, Esq.

### Borough of *Kells*.

Patrick Everard, Esq. ;
John Delamare, Esq.

### Borough of *Ratoath*.

John Hussey, Esq. ;
James Fitzgerald, Esq.

### County of MONAGHAN.

Bryan MacMahon, Esq., 9th July, 1689 ;
Hugh MacMahon, Esq., 9th July, 1689.

### QUEEN'S COUNTY.

Sir Patrick Trant, Knight ;
Edmond Morres, Esq.

### Borough of *Maryborough*.

Pierce Bryan, Esq. ;
Thady Fitzpatrick, Esq.

### Borough of *Ballynakill*.

Sir Gregory Byrne, Bart. ;
Oliver Grace, Esq.

### Borough of *Portarlington*.

Sir Henry Bond, Bart. ;
Sir Thomas Hacket, Knight.

### County of ROSCOMMON.

Charles Kelly, Esq. ;
John Bourk, Esq.

### Borough of *Roscommon*.

John Dillon, Esq. ;
John Kelly, Esq.

APPENDIX. 167

### Borough of *Boyle*.
Captain John King ;
Terence MacDermot, Alderman ; 6th May, 1639.

### County of SLIGO.
Henry Crofton, Esq, ;
Oliver O'Gara, Esq.

### Borough of *Sligo*.
Terence MacDonogh, Esq.; 8th May, 1689 ;
James French, Esq. ; 8th May, 1689.

### County of TIPPERARY.
Nicholas Purcel, of Loghmore, Esq. ;
James Butler, of Grangebeg, Esq.

### Borough of *Clonmel*.
Nicholas White, Alderman ;
John Bray, Alderman.

### City of *Cashel*.
Dennis Kearny, Alderman ;
James Hacket, Alderman.

### Borough of *Feathard*.
Sir John Everard, Bart. ;
James Tobin, of Feathard, Esq.

### County of TYRONE.
Colonel Gordon O'Neill ;
Lewis Doe, of Dungannon, Esq.

### Borough of *Dungannon*.
Arthur O'Neill, of Ballygawley, Esq. ;
Peter Donnelly, of Dungannon, Esq.

### Borough of *Strabane*.
Christypher Nugent, of Dublin, Esq, ;
Daniel Donnelly, of the same, Gent. 8th May, 1689.

### County of WATERFORD.

John Power, Esq. ;
Matthew Hore, Esq.

### City of *Waterford*.

John Porter, Esq. ;
Nicholas Fitzgerald, Esq.

### Borough of *Dungarvan*.

John Hore, Esq. ; 7th May, 1689 ;
Martin Hore, Esq.; 7th May, 1689.

### County of WESTMEATH.

The Honorable Colonel William Nugent ;
The Honorable Colonel Henry Dillon.

### Borough of *Athlone*.

Edmond Malone, of Ballynahoune, Esq. ;
Edmond Malone, Esq. ; Counsellor at Law.

### Borough of *Kilbeggan*.

Bryan Geoghegan, of Donore, Esq. ;
Charles Geoghegan, of Lyonane, Esq.

### Manor of *Mullingar*.

Gerard Dillon, Esq. ; Prime-Sergeant ;
Edmond Nugent, of Carlanstown, Esq.

### Borough of *Fore*.

John Nugent, of Donore, Esq. ;
Christopher Nugent, of Dardystown, Esq.

### County of WEXFORD.

Walter Butler, of Munfine, Esq. ;
Patrick Colclough, of Mochury, Esq.

### Town of *Wexford*.

William Talbot, Esq. ;
Francis Rooth, Merchant.

### Town of *New Ross*.

Luke Dormer, Esq. ;
Richard Butler, Esq.

### Borough of *Enniscorthy*.

James Devereux, of Carrigmenan, Esq. ;
Dudley Colclough, of Moughery, Esq. ;
Arthur Waddington, Esq., Portreeve, by a new election.

### Borough of *Fethard*.

The Right Honorable Colonel James Porter :
Captain Nicholas Stafford.

### Borough of *Newborough*, alias *Gorey*.

Abraham Strange, of Toberduff, Esq.;
Richard Doyle, of Kilorky, Esq.

### Borough of *Bannow*.

Francis Plowden, Esq. ; Commissioner of the Revenues ;
Dr. Alexis Stafford.

### Borough of *Clomines*.

Edward Sherlock, of the City of Dublin, Esq. ;
Nicholas White, of New Ross, Merhant.

### Borough of *Taghmon*.

George Hore, of Polehore, Esq. ;
Walter Hoer, of Harperstown, Esq.

### County of WICKLOW.

Richard Butler, Esq.;
William Talbot, Esq.

### Borough of *Wicklow*.

Francis Toole, Esq. ;
Thomas Byrne, Esq.

### Borough of *Carysfort.*

Hugh Byrne, Esq. ;
Pierce Archbold, Esq. ; upon whose default of appearance ;
Bartholomew Polewheele, Esq.

### Borough of *Blessington.*

James Eustace, Esq. ;
Maurice Eustace, Gent.

*The Commons choose Sir* Richard Nagle *their Speaker, and Mr.* John Kerney *was Clerk of that House.*

---

# APPENDIX B.

## ALEXANDER FITTON, CHANCELLOR OF IRELAND.

King's statement about Fitton's "detection of forgery," and imprisonment—in which King has, of course, been followed blindly by Hume, Macaulay and other writers on the same side ever since—is, as Davis suspected, entirely misleading.

Alexander Fitton was descended from Sir Edward Fitton, Kt. of Gosworth, Cheshire (ob. 1579), who was Treasurer of Ireland and President of Connaught and Thomond. The senior branch of the family became extinct with Sir Edward Fitton, Bart., of Gosworth (great-grandson of the Treasurer), who died s.p. in 1643. By a deed executed in 1642 the estates, after Lady Fitton's death, passed to the younger branch, settled in Ireland, then represented by William Fitton of Awne, father of Alexander. William only got possession of them after three law suits with the sisters of Sir Edward Fitton.

Nearly 20 years later, when Alexander had succeeded to the property, the estates were claimed by Lord Brandon (afterwards

Earl of Macclesfield) whose mother Penelope was a sister of Sir Edward Fitton, and who exhibited a will in his favour, then heard of for the first time. Alexander Fitton then produced a deed poll, dated 1643, which confirmed the deed of 1642 and would have nullified the alleged will. Lord Brandon declared that the deed poll was a forgery, and produced (from gaol) a witness named Granger who swore he had forged it at Alexander Fitton's instigation. His story was backed by witnesses only to this extent, that they swore they had heard Alexander Fitton declare that he had paid Granger £40 to forge a deed for him—a circumstance about which one can hardly believe that Fitton would have been so communicative. On the other hand, witnesses were produced who swore that they had *seen* the deed before the date alleged for the forgery. The jury, probably not uninfluenced by the fact that Fitton had turned Catholic while Lord Brandon was a strong Protestant and Royalist found that the deed poll was a forgery and gave Lord Brandon the estates. Subsequently Granger retracted his whole story in a printed document, but as the document contained violent charges against Lord Brandon the House of Lords took the matter up, laid hold of Alexander Fitton, and sentenced him to pay a fine of £500 and lie in prison till he should produce Granger, which he could not or would not do.

It appears therefore (1) that Fitton was not imprisoned for forgery but for publishing a vindication of himself; (2) that the evidence for the forgery rests entirely on Granger's testimony; (3) that this testimony is perfectly worthless for any purpose. The fact that the deed poll of 1643 was not produced until the deed of 1642 was met by the alleged will, shows only common prudence on the Fittons' part. They knew the other side to be determined and perhaps unscrupulous, and it was their obvious policy not to show more of their hand than they could help.

Ormerod ("Hist. of Cheshire," III. 290 ff.) seems to suspect that the will under which Lord Brandon claimed was a forgery and that the deed poll may have been a counter-forgery to meet it. But Oliver Burke (" Lives of the Chancellors") holds that Fitton was wrongfully dispossessed, defamed and punished, and so I think will the impartial student. It is certainly not surprising that King James thought so; and indeed it is clear that the most arbitrary of kings could not have raised such a man to such a position unless the conviction of his innocence had been strong and general. There is a rare tract in the British Museum published in Fitton's defence in 1663 and entitled "A true Narrative of the Proceedings in the several Suits in Law that have been between Rt. Hon. Charles Lord Gerard of Brandon and Alex. Fitton. Esq. By a Lover of Truth." It contains Granger's recantation.

T. W. R.

www.ingramcontent.com/pod-product-compliance
Lightning Source LLC
Chambersburg PA
CBHW032138230426
43672CB00011B/2372